This book is dedicated to my friend, while fighting for his

An old photograph. A baby's laugh. An old T-shirt hanging in the closet. It's funny how the insignificant things in life can carry such weight in our hearts. For me, it is the wind rushing through the windows of a brown Cutlass speeding down the streets of Hereford, Texas, with Bon Jovi blaring through the noise of the wind. It's a smile and the laughter of a good friend as we travel down the road. When I think back on my days of hanging out with Jason, I can't really recall earthshaking moments the way I can in memories of my wife or my children. But the seemingly insignificant things draw tears from my eyes and create an ache in my heart. It is the small things in our friendship that mean so much to me. I miss my friend.

In my mind, I can still see him laughing, and I always will. Men always retain inside of them the boy they once were, but as life flows on, year after year, adult issues take precedence. Driving too fast, listening to too-loud music, and singing way off-key to Bon Jovi would give way to talks of fear, destiny, and eternity. The run-down Cutlass was replaced by a dignified Land Rover. The jabs, jokes, and zingers never stopped, but they were enclosed by words of God, regret, legacy, and great hope. I think that was the spirit we fostered in one another: great hope. We believed God, and we believed that all things were possible.

We believed in one another to the end. His faith in me and my faith in him interlaced our hearts together more than our escapades in Hereford, Texas, ever could. His faith in me helped me to write this book. I hope my faith in him helped him to keep fighting. I suppose, when so many had accepted the inevitable, he was still looking for a better treatment, and I was still praying for his healing.

And if you think about it, I suppose his quest and my prayers both found their way. He received a treatment that removed all cancer, and he is completely and totally healed. I celebrate his faith in Jesus Christ. I celebrate his place in heaven before our heavenly Father. I celebrate the memories. I celebrate, but my eyes water and my heart hurts. I miss my friend.

1

Contents

Chapter 1

Noble Plans

Tomorrow

Looking back is easy. At least, it's easier to see what God *was* doing when we look back in time than it is to guess what He *will* do in the future. There have been so many times in my life when what I was doing at the moment did not make sense. I would ask the Lord what He was doing. I would ask what He was trying to teach me. Many times I would say to the Lord, "If you will just tell me what the lesson is, I will gladly learn it and accept it, and then we can move on."

But too often, I did not even know what I was supposed to learn. All I knew was that God was at work. I knew this mainly because it was what I had heard from so many pastors and evangelists in my life. I knew God was working on me somehow, but I was confused. I was dazed. I was frustrated and ready to give up, because I just could not understand what was happening.

After some time passed, things were much clearer. Sometimes, it would be the next day. Other times, years went by before I could look back and understand what God was trying to teach me or do in me or for me. Looking back is much easier than looking a dilemma in the face and wondering what in the world God is doing. Even worse is wondering, *What should I do?*

As a pastor, I hear this question often. People will come into my office and spill their guts, telling me everything that is going on in their lives. They give me every detail of every situation, and then, after a long time, they finally take a breath and say, "What should I do?" These conversations revolve around everything under the sun. *Should I leave my husband? Should I take this job or stay where I am? Is God calling me into ministry?* It goes on and on. Tomorrow seems like such a mystery. And trying to figure out what we should do—whether in certain situations or for the direction of our lives—can be frustrating.

What is tomorrow? What should it be? What should it look like? What does God say about tomorrow? The questions of relationships, career, family, and church can be so difficult. What is God's plan for your tomorrow, and for all the tomorrows of your life? Let's consider what the Lord says to us about tomorrow:

> Now listen, you who say, "Today or tomorrow we will go to this or that city, spend a year there, carry on business and make money." Why, you do not even know what will happen tomorrow. What is your life? You are a mist that appears for a little while and then vanishes. Instead, you ought to say, "If it is the Lord's will, we will live and do this or that." As it is, you boast in your arrogant schemes. All such boasting is evil. If anyone, then, knows the good they ought to do and doesn't do it, it is sin for them. (James 4:13–17 NIV)

When we first read this Scripture, it is teaching us that we should not worry about tomorrow. It is even teaching that we should not make any plans. However, the Scripture also teaches us that the "noble man makes noble plans" (Isaiah 32:8). So, Isaiah is teaching us that if we are going to be noble, with a desire to live our lives producing fruit, we should make plans. We should consider tomorrow and make plans. How do we reconcile these two different thoughts that seem to contradict one another?

The point of the Scripture in James is that we should not take tomorrow for granted. We don't know if we are going to be here tomorrow. Haven't we been shocked and surprised when someone suddenly passes away by sickness or tragedy? Yet in spite of our surprise, the truth is that this is life. There is no guarantee for tomorrow. James was teaching us that tomorrow is not a given, and we should not assume that we will be able to do this or that tomorrow. Instead, we should be making noble plans. We should live each day, making the most of our lives. We should plan lives filled with noble things, compassionate things, excellent things—things that will last even when we have expired.

Too many Christians live life as if they have plenty of time to do great things tomorrow. They encounter each morning with a nonchalant attitude, not really having direction or purpose. When we do not plan, aren't we taking tomorrow for granted? Aren't we living life as if it does not matter? Aren't we assuming that we will have more time to realize the plans for our lives? Day after day, week after week, month after month, year after year, time goes by, and we never really do anything with our lives. To settle for an insignificant life is not only a waste; it is sinful.

"For this very reason, make every effort to add to your faith goodness; and to goodness, knowledge; and to knowledge, self-control; and to self-control, perseverance; and to perseverance, godliness; and to godliness, brotherly kindness; and to brotherly kindness, love. For if you possess these qualities in increasing measure, they will keep you from being ineffective and unproductive in your knowledge of our Lord Jesus Christ. But if anyone does not have them, he is nearsighted and blind, and has forgotten that he has been cleansed from his past sins" (2 Peter 1:5–9 NIV).

Each one of us, as a believer, has been designated as God's mouthpiece to the world. An invisible God has chosen you to reveal Him to people in a physical world. What a calling! What an honorable position! I know, I know, most people don't think that way. They think that God reveals Himself through pastors and teachers, at church and on television.

But this is so far from the truth! God is a personal God. He reaches people right where they are. And we are His missionaries, sent into all of the world to make disciples of Jesus Christ. There are some people in your life who only know one solid Christian—you. What will you do with this responsibility?

God's plan for us, however, is about more than evangelism. He has called us to help the needy, to take care of widows and orphans, to clothe the naked, feed the hungry, and care for the sick. But wait! His plan involves more than just service. You have people under your care, be it a spouse, children, or others. God has called you to provide for them financially, spiritually, emotionally, physically, and socially. You have been created to make a difference and to have an impact. That impact involves more than just the people you come into contact with. God has given you influence over situations that will affect others—people at work, your neighbors, your church, or people around the world. God has great plans for you!

"'For I know the plans I have for you,' declares the Lord, 'plans to prosper you and not to harm you, plans to give you hope and a future'" (Jeremiah 29:11 NIV). We have all read or heard this verse a thousand times. But read it again. Let it sink into your spirit. Don't think for a minute that this does not apply to you. God says that He knew you before He formed your body in the womb of your mom. All of your days have been ordained, and each day of your life has a purpose. God has a plan for each day, and that plan is sometimes a mystery, but it is a mystery within the confines of this passage. No matter what God's plan is for your life, it includes prosperity, protection, hope, and a future. Praise God!

I want to challenge you to make some noble plans for your life. The word *noble* means "free." It comes from a time when only those of a higher social class were free. Slaves and servants did not always have the freedom to do what they wanted. However, the nobility were free to do as they wanted.

God has made you noble (Exodus 19:6). You are noble, and you are free. You are free today to make your life whatever you want it to be. You are not confined by anything, anyone, or any circumstance. You are not restrained by people, money, or influence. You are not stifled because of your past, your wounds, or your pain. Through it all, you are free to make life what you want it to be. This freedom can get you into trouble if you do not include God in the equation, but you do have freedom to make your life what you want it to be.

Tomorrow is a mystery, but what grand potential every day holds for those who set forth a path of noble plans. Do not let another day just slip by without accomplishing something great or setting the stage to do something great. Don't take tomorrow for granted. Plan to make it count!

The Place I Will Show You

> The Lord had said to Abram, "Go from your country, your
> people and your father's household to the land I will show you. I
> will make you into a great nation, and I will bless you; I will
> make your name great, and you will be a blessing. I will bless
> those who bless you, and whoever curses you I will curse; and all
> peoples on earth will be blessed through you." So Abram went,
> as the Lord had told him; and Lot went with him. Abram was
> seventy-five years old when he set out from Harran. He took his
> wife Sarai, his nephew Lot, all the possessions they had
> accumulated and the people they had acquired in Harran, and
> they set out for the land of Canaan, and they arrived there.
> (Genesis 12:1–5 NIV)

It is so easy to miss the significance of this passage of Scripture. God
laid out this wonderful plan for Abram and his family to be blessed and
protected beyond what they could ever imagine. But God told Abram to
go to a place that He would show him. He didn't tell Abram where he
was going, and He didn't even promise that Abram would be able to
keep the land that God was going to take him to. The only promise was
that God would "show" him the land.

So Abram gathered all of his family and their possessions—along with
his nephew Lot, who was probably somewhat like a son—and they left.
The book of Hebrews speaks of Abram's obedience, though he had no
idea where he was going. He just packed up and left. Can you imagine
packing up all of your belongings into a giant U-Haul truck or two,
loading the kids into the truck, leaving family and friends, and driving
off—without any idea where you are going? This was a tremendous act
of obedience.

Abram did not argue. He did not back away. He did not roll his eyes or rebel. He was not passive aggressive. He just went. God said, "Go!" and Abram went.

Before we begin to make plans of our own, our first step should be to ask God what His plans are for us. We can make plans all day long, but unless God is in them, we will work toward these goals in vain. Without God's guidance, our goals will not accomplish what we hope they will. They will not give us peace, prosperity, or blessing. These plans that we make for ourselves and go after in our own will may sometimes look like a great blessing. But in time we will see that these seemingly wonderful blessings have ensnared us and trapped us in a lifestyle we do not want.

Too often, we make our plans and tell God, "This is the plan. Here is what I am going to do." Then we ask God to bless the plans that we made for ourselves rather than ask God what His plans are—even though we know that His plans for us are already blessed because they come from Him.

It is really quite audacious for us to assume that we know the best path for our lives. We have no clue what is going to happen tomorrow, but we have a God who has already existed in every tomorrow of our lives. He knows the hardships that we will face. He knows the flow of the markets, when they will rise and when they will fall. He knows the blessings He plans to bestow upon us, and He knows which of these we will receive and which we will reject. He is not surprised by wars, storms, or global financial meltdowns. He knows it all, and He promises to go before us and open doors of blessing and close doors that would lead us down the wrong paths.

Ask Him. Go ahead. Ask, "Lord, what are Your plans for me and my life? Where should I go? What should I do?" And wait for His answer.

Abram eventually made it to the place God had for Him. We are told in Scripture how God guided and directed him every step of the way until he settled in what would be the Promised Land. If only we could live within the promise of His guidance, imagine how much less we would worry and stress out. We are so afraid of the unknown, but we serve a God who knows all. I accept not knowing what tomorrow holds, because

He is my guide. He will lead me forward, whether the way is blessed or difficult, and I can rest in that. I do not have to live in fear of thoughts like, *I hope this happens* or *I hope that does not happen.*

Going one step further, God promises that whatever we face, good or bad, He will work out toward our good. He will use it to make us better people, better fathers, and better mothers. No matter what happens, I am going to be all right, as long as I keep my faith in Jesus Christ. The peace we experience transcends understanding. It bewilders people and give us the opportunity to give Him glory.

Right now, as you consider your future, stop worrying. Stop stressing. Stop being anxious. So what if you don't know what to do or where to go or who to hang on to or let go of. No worries. Your God in heaven does know what you should do, and in time, when it is time, He will guide your next step. Step by step with God, you will overcome every obstacle and every pain, and little by little, His most glorious plan for your life will fall into place.

Our Purpose

Sometimes we have a tendency to look at the world as if we are the center of it and the world revolves around us. This is in part a design by God. When we are children, we must assume that the world revolves around us, or we may not make our needs known to our caregivers. If a baby is not persistent about crying when hungry or thirsty or having a full diaper, these needs may not be met in a timely manner.

But as we grow up, we must change the way we think. The world does not revolve around us. I know that some of us struggle with the shock of learning that there is life in the universe outside of us, but trust me, it is true. You and I are not the center of the universe. This means, of course, that your thoughts, your plans, and your desires are not the most important things going on at any given time. We have to stop making plans as if our thoughts, dreams, and desires are the number-one priority of this earth.

We were brought into existence by a Creator with a purpose. Our purpose is not to be a teacher, a policeman, a businesswoman, or anything else. Our purpose is not even to be a mom, dad, or big brother. All of these relationships and goals are important, but they are not your purpose. These are not what you were created for. They may fit into the purpose for which you were created, but they themselves are not the purpose.

To fully understand this, we must first gain a greater comprehension of the nature of God. God created you and me, along with the whole human race. But why? Why did He create us? What was His purpose in doing so? Why has He created so many of us? There are six billion people on the earth, I am told, and that is just today. What about all of the people who have populated this earth since Adam and Eve? What is God's purpose?

One thing we know is that God does not *need* us. He is self-sufficient. He is not lonely. He is not afraid of the dark of the universe and does not need someone to talk to when he is afraid. He does not need us. Maybe we could say that He *wants* us. That could have some validity, because He loves us. But there are many people who are going to reject God and spend eternity in hell. And the strange part about this is that God knows which people are going to decide to reject Him—before they are even born. If that's the case, why not just *not* create them?

Linear time is not an issue for God. He already knows the decisions that we and all of the human race will make concerning our faith in Him. In spite of this knowledge, God does whatever He can to move us toward Him anyway. Although I do believe that God *wants* us, I don't believe that is the reason for His continual propagation of the human race. There are too many being born each and every day who will, and do, reject Him.

God is by nature a community. Therefore, His nature is to constantly produce community. He is life. He is always giving life and creating life, not because He needs us, nor because He is lonely, but because He is community. Father, Son, and Holy Spirit are the original community, but by nature, they give life to further the community. Revelation teaches us that after Christ comes back, during the millennium, Satan will be kept in captivity, but after the thousand years, he will be set free to deceive

11

people. This means that even after the rapture, during the millennium, God will still continue to produce more and more people. It is His nature.

It is also His nature to love. Love and community go together. Because He loves, He gives life. Because He gives life, He loves the life that He gives. As a community, God is always producing more, but He loves and wants all those He has created. Because He loves the human race, He does not force us to love Him in return. If He forced us to love Him or created us in such a way that we did not have a choice, we could not say that He truly loved us.

True love does not force itself on anyone. It loves, even when unrequited, hoping that in the face of this great love, the object will one day return this love. It is God's hope that He can reveal Himself and the love He has for all people, so that all might be ushered into heaven, welcomed into the community of believers, into the family of God where He is the great Patriarch. People will continue to be born, even those who will not choose God. But He loves each one of us anyway and does everything He can to reach the entire human race, because He does not desire for any human being to go to hell—even though many will.

Once we understand this, and the nature of God, we must see everything through His perspective.

Perhaps you want to be a musician or a professional athlete. How does that fit into the plan of the God who placed you into the womb of your mother in a particular society during a particular time of the ages? These are things you did not choose. He could have let you be born into a people or culture so long ago that there was no such thing as a "professional" anything. Then your purpose might have seemed different to you, because life would have been different. Our purpose as people, created by God, does not change. You were born for this time at this moment. Why?

We have been made in the image of God. He is a creator, and I would suggest to you that on a much diminished scale, so are we. We create. Our words and our actions mold those we have influence over. Our actions and words can give someone hope or tear someone down. We help them heal, or we hurt them worse. We give them a new perspective, or we continue to beat them up over their past. We bless people. We curse people. We help them come to life, or we kill them time and again. In every relationship we have, we are creating something in others. It may be big or small, good or bad, significant or not, but we are all influenced by the people we interact with, and this continual rubbing together of souls does affect us.

Your purpose is connected to your influence. By nature, you have influence and will always have influence. Even someone who is a total introvert still influences people when he interacts with them—or is unable to interact with them. Our closest relationships are where we carry the greatest influence, creating life or death, blessings or curses in people.

This influence is by design. God has created you in His image so that you might also create life in others. This is how He reveals Himself to the creation He desires to spend eternity with. He is an unseen God, and He uses us to reveal Himself to a world that can't see Him. The Holy Spirit works through us to bring glory to God. When we live a life of love and give God glory, we influence others toward God, which allows Him to influence them toward eternal life. When He blesses us and we give Him glory, people are watching. When we go through the valleys of life but have some kind of strength or peace that surpasses all understanding, people notice and take note that we are believers in Jesus Christ.

Here is the kicker: all people will bring glory to God. Those who believe and trust in Him will bring Him glory when people witness their blessings, their strength, their ability to forgive, their joy, their patience, and so on. These believers will give glory to God. But God will also receive glory through Satan-worshippers. Though a person like this might degrade God to those around him, the Satan-worshipper will eventually receive the wrath of God on this earth, and his life will not be attractive to anyone. The curses in his life, combined with his testimony against God, will cause people to put two and two together. Those who choose Christ will be blessed, and those who don't will be cursed.

I have especially seen this in ministry as a hospice chaplain. You only have to walk into two different homes where someone is dying. Though there is sadness in the home of believers, there is also joy and hope. In a home where the family does not have a strong belief in Christ, there is an overwhelming sadness combined with a total absence of hope.

When we see the combination of people in our lives—those who are living for God and experiencing His blessing, and those who are living contrary to God and living under curses—God paints a picture for all to see: that the only way to fulfillment, joy, peace, and love is through Jesus Christ and no other.

Still Standing

When God called to Abram, He used his name. So, what's the big deal about that? I know it sounds simple, but it is quite profound. Before we get too far into this, consider this Scripture from the Psalms: "For you created my inmost being; you knit me together in my mother's womb. I praise you because I am fearfully and wonderfully made; your works are wonderful, I know that full well. My frame was not hidden from you when I was made in the secret place. When I was woven together in the depths of the earth, your eyes saw my unformed body. All the days ordained for me were written in your book before one of them came to be" (Psalm 139:13–16 NIV).

This is such a powerful Scripture. It teaches us that all of our days were ordained and written in God's book before we were ever born. The word *ordained* says that there is a purpose. There is a plan. God's plans for you did not begin when you were born. They will not end for you when you die. The plans that God has for you never change.

Without a doubt, it is our choice to follow His plans or not, but He never lets go of His plans for us. He never stops dreaming for us. He never stops hoping for us. Many of us might think to ourselves that because of our sin or sinful lifestyle, God might give up on us and His plans for us. Let me be God's mouthpiece for just a moment and let you know that God *never* gives up on us. The plans that He designed for us before we were born are always there waiting for us. Even our sin does not erase what He has written in His book about our lives.

Consider Abram. Abram's name was orchestrated by God, because every day we have on this earth has purpose, and names are important to God. The word *Abram* means "high father." Abram, however, was in his old age and still did not have a child. This was not a society in which some people decided to not have children. This was a society in which success and blessing were judged by the number of children a person had. Abram might even have felt that he was under some kind of curse because he had no children. He had somewhat adopted his nephew Lot, but he had no children of his own. He was named "father," but he lived a childless life.

But God had a plan that involved an appointed time. God never gives up on us. We must never give up on Him. If we don't see anything from God, we must not assume that He has forgotten about us or discarded us. That is a lie from hell. We must wait and keep our faith, and at the appointed time, His plans for our lives will come to life.

Because Abram's days were ordained by God and written in His book—as are our days—God was not surprised when Abram went to Egypt and told a lie. Being afraid for his own life, Abram told Pharaoh that Sarai was his sister, which was partially true, but it was still an attempt to deceive.

Even so, God was not shocked. He did not suddenly start having heart palpitations. Before Abram was born, God had been aware that he would commit that sin on that very day for the very reason he did it, but God had a purpose for it. He intended to use the situation as a moment of discipline to teach Abram to walk more faithfully in obedience to Him. God had called Abram by his name since before he was born. The plans that God had for him would not go away just because he sinned.

God's plan for our lives is not waiting to be written. If so, God would have looked at our future sin and erased His blessings for us, but our sin does not negate His plans. Those plans have been written by the hand of God, in the book of God, for all of the angels to read, whenever they step into heaven's library. It is a book of the future and the past, all at the same time, because every detail of every part of our lives is already known to God.

In spite of knowing every lie you would tell and every wrong you would do, God still established plans for you. Before you ever cheated, lied, stole money, slept around, got high, played church, pretended to be something you weren't, or corrupted your heart, He established a plan for you. Nothing you do can erase it. You can postpone it, delay it, or avoid it, but praise God, you can never erase it! Though you run from it all of your life, when you finally come to your senses—whether you are nineteen or ninety—His plans are right there. He loves you and dreams for you. Despite anything in your life that might make you think His plan for you is over, it's never over. He's just waiting.

The extent to which God loves us and has planned a wonderful life for us—even knowing every horrible sin we will commit—melts our hearts. It softens us to Him, because no one else will ever love us like this. Sometimes people give up on us quickly and easily. They see our weaknesses, our failures, and our pasts, and they decide that we will never do or become anything worthwhile in our lives. But while they are running us into the ground, we must tune our hearts toward heaven.

"Ha!"

Did you hear that? Ha! That's God talking! To all of those voices that have tried to convince you that you are nothing, God screams from His throne at them: "Ha! I showed you!" This is what He says to all of your critics and enemies, to those who hate you. He loves to declare this to the people in your life who have dismissed you, put you down, set you aside, pushed you down, and discarded you. From heaven thunders a booming voice for both demons and angels to hear. "Ha!"

The demons hear it. All of your life, they have spent their energy trying to surround you with these kinds of people, doing everything possible to undermine your confidence and destroy you, but you are still standing. *You are still standing!*

When you started reading this book, it may have been the first time in a long time that you decided to see what God wanted for your life. You may not see that God's plans for your life have come to pass at all, but the fact that you picked up this book and are reading it now is a roundhouse kick to the face of Satan. As he hits the canvas, God is in his face, shouting, "Ha!"

Let this be your victory cry to let every spirit, every enemy, every doubter, and every hater know that you are still standing. They might have knocked you down, but you didn't stay down. They may have hit you hard, but they did not knock you out. And even if today is your first day back in the plans of God, here you are … still standing. They didn't win. They will never win. They have been defeated. "Ha!"

Even Greater Things

> When Abram was ninety-nine years old, the Lord appeared to him and said, "I am God Almighty; walk before me and be blameless. I will confirm my covenant between me and you and will greatly increase your numbers." Abram fell facedown, and God said to him, "As for me, this is my covenant with you: You will be the father of many nations. No longer will you be called Abram; your name will be Abraham, for I have made you a father of many nations. I will make you very fruitful; I will make nations of you, and kings will come from you." (Genesis 17:1–6 NIV)

God had ordained each day of Abram's life. Though Abram's name came through a mother or father, it was a name ordained by God. *Abram* means "high father," and God's plan for him had been established long before he was born. Abram was to be a father.

Here in this passage, we see God coming to Abram and changing his name to *Abraham*, which means "father of nations." At this point, Abraham had only one son, and that son was not even the son of God's promise who would be the heir of these great plans that God had for Abram. His son Ishmael was not old enough to be married. There were no grandchildren. Even before the first part of God's plan for Abram was anywhere near complete, God augmented that plan, saying that Abram was going to be a "father of nations."

God's plans for your life are bigger than the person you are right now. Perhaps God has begun to show you His plans. Maybe you are beginning to see the fruit of those plans, and some things are beginning to happen. Well, before you get too far along, I want you to know that the plans God has revealed to you so far are only a drop in the bucket. He has greater plans for you that have not yet been revealed. Wherever you are at in your walk with the Lord, His plans for you involve so much more than what you have seen. As your life moves further into His plans for you, He will augment those plans. He will lead you as far as He can. He dreams big!

God's plans for our lives are so wonderful that if He gave them to us before we were ready, the blessings themselves would become a temptation. We would be tempted to worship the blessings themselves. God could give us the most wonderful job or the most wonderful person as a spouse, but if we are not mature enough in our walk with Him, these good things, these blessings, would become a snare. Therefore, God has to mature us. We might also become arrogant if we received such blessing too quickly. So God has to prepare our hearts to be able to receive such wondrous things without making them our god or becoming so arrogant that we somehow think we have produced them ourselves.

Mmmm. I can hear you now. You're thinking, *Well, I have earned some blessings in this life. I worked hard and earned a promotion. I saved and earned a new home. I am responsible for many of the good things in my life.* Consider this: You could have been born in Haiti. You could have been born without mental abilities. You could have been born into circumstances that would not have allowed a blessing like this to take place.

I remember preaching at a youth retreat where the Lord was really reaching the hearts of teenagers. Between services, I thought to myself, *I am really preaching well.* It was an arrogant thought. I never would have *said* that these teenagers were responding so well because of me, but my innermost thoughts were arrogant and conceited.

God said to me, *Why are you thinking so highly of yourself? There is nothing that you or any other preacher could ever say that has not already been said by another preacher, and all of it comes from the Holy Spirit anyway. I have shared it with you so that you can share it with them.*

I realized that a preacher was just a spiritual plagiarist. All I could do was take the words of the Holy Spirit and restate them. There was nothing original in my thoughts that had not already been said by someone—and if not by someone else, then by God Himself. Who was I to take credit for anything?

No matter what we might think, every good and perfect gift comes from above. Every blessing in our lives comes from God.

I am not saying that you did not work hard or that your intelligence did not help you. I am saying that the opportunities you have are in some way dependent upon the providence of God, either before you were born or since. Your ability to see, to walk, to think, and even to breathe is evidence of the faithfulness of God. All the days of your life have been ordained by God. He chose you. He chose your parents. He chose your nation of origin. He chose your health at birth. Not everyone is born with working limbs. Not everyone is born with the ability to see. Not everyone has full mental faculties. Not everyone has the same opportunities for education. Not everyone gets to live as long as you have. Every good and perfect gift is from above.

Maybe, just maybe, this is one of the lessons you need to learn. If, for any reason, you are now taking credit for anything good in your life, how can the Lord trust you not to become more arrogant with more blessing? Though we put forth effort, we are only planting seeds. It is the Lord who gives the increase. You can work hard, but if your boss thinks you are lazy, your efforts mean nothing. If you work in a political atmosphere where the only people who are blessed are part of a certain group, how did you suddenly get a promotion? It is the Lord's doing, of course.

Though you are enjoying some of the blessings of God's plan for your life, He is just getting started. Even if you have lived all of your life with Him and in His plans, He is *still* just getting started. The blessings you have enjoyed have not somehow made you exempt from hardship. The issues and problems have still been there, and you have had to endure. With each battle comes a new lesson. You may be struggling right now, not because God has given up on you but because He is preparing and maturing you to be able to receive greater plans and greater blessings without falling in love with the blessings or yourself.

When life stinks and everything goes wrong, give Him praise. He is increasing your destiny and expanding His dream for you. Don't give up during the hard times. He has found you worthy of more than what you have now. And get ready, because He is just getting started. He is changing your name. He is reaching deeper into His pockets for a greater plan. These plans are so awesome that you are not even ready for them yet. He has to teach you how to walk more strongly, stand more firmly, worship more wildly, and humble yourself more. Start praising Him now for what is on the other side of these lessons. It is truly more than you have ever seen or heard, more than you could ever conceive—just as the Scripture has said.

The hardest part about God's plan for your life is the way He prepares you to live in it. Think about it. The blessings alone are so wonderful that some of you might begin to think so highly of the blessings that they overshadow your love for God Himself. Those must be some great plans. He wants to bless you without corrupting you. He wants to give you everything, but He doesn't want you to be like a spoiled little kid who acts as if people owe him everything. He wants to give you the world without your thinking that you own the world.

The truth is that His plans for you are wonderful and amazing. But you must absolutely understand that the person you are today is not ready, not mature enough, to handle His plans. You must be willing, and even eager, to be crafted and molded into what you need to be for His plans. Most of us would say, "Yes, Lord, these plans are so wonderful that I give you permission to change anything about me that needs to be changed." Right? Most of us would agree to the difficulties, since they are the pathway to these wonderful plans for our lives. It is not God's intent that we disagree with. We rather like His intent. The Bible says that He wants to give us good gifts. No, it's not God's intent that we struggle with. It's His methodology.

We must remember that Scripture teaches a very strange thing about Christ being perfected: "In bringing many sons and daughters to glory, it was fitting that God, for whom and through whom everything exists, should make the pioneer of their salvation perfect through what he suffered" (Hebrews 2:10 NIV). This is such a strange Scripture. It teaches us that Christ was made perfect through suffering. But wasn't He already perfect?

God had to *show* that Christ was perfect. It had to be clear that Christ was without sin in his behavior so that we would be justified by His death. Had Christ sinned, then His crucifixion would only have been the punishment due for His own sin. He had to remain perfect so He could receive, as a man, punishment that He did not deserve. Because He did not deserve punishment Himself, He alone was worthy to hang on that cross in our place. This Scripture teaches us that His perfection was proven. It was clearly established and made visible through His suffering. He lived as a man, completely dependent on the Holy Spirit.

This is why the Scripture says that He was tempted in every way. The only way He could be tempted was if he had a sinful nature. A divine nature cannot be tempted by sin or evil, but Christ was tempted in every way (Hebrews 4:15). So, though we know He lived a perfect life, it was the suffering and His response to the suffering that proved His perfection. When we see Him hanging on the cross, saying, "Father, forgive them, for they know not what they do," His perfection is made clear (Luke 23:34).

Therefore, we understand suffering to be the vehicle by which we are able to measure our spiritual maturity. I can tell how much I have grown by the way I respond to suffering. We are called to consider it pure joy when we suffer. We are taught to remain positive, to forgive, and to continue praising, even as we suffer. We are to consider it an honor that the Devil considers us worthy of being attacked.

Is this how you respond? Do you get angry or hold a grudge when someone attacks you, or do Christ's words also come out of your mouth: "Father, forgive them"? The degree of your maturity can be measured by comparing your most recent response to suffering to your previous responses. If you want to see how you are doing, evaluate your reaction to your spouse the next time he or she offends you, and compare it to the last time. Have you grown?

If you are still responding to difficult issues in the same way you always have, it really doesn't matter how many times you have been to church or how many Sunday school lessons you have taught or how many people have come to the altar in response to your sermon. Even a preacher can perfect his communication skills without growing spiritually. Just because you have a gift from the Holy Spirit does not mean that you are producing the fruit of the Spirit.

This is why God's methodology is difficult. His methodology allows Satan to attack us, just as He gave Satan permission to attack Christ and Job and Paul and Silas and … we could go on forever. Suffering. Trials. Tribulation. These are our measuring sticks to see what we need to work on.

Do I worry too much and need to work on living by faith? Do I hold a grudge and need to forgive more fully? Am I jealous of what others have and need to learn contentment? Am I brash and need to learn self-control? Am I greedy and need to learn generosity? Am I judgmental and need to learn compassion? These questions are answered when we respond to our suffering.

As long as I despise suffering, my anger toward that which is causing my suffering will keep me from stepping back to evaluate my response, and I will never learn and never grow. I must learn to value suffering. I must see beyond the suffering itself to what God is trying to reveal to me about myself. These lessons are key, if I am to grow into the person who can handle God's most wonderful plans for me.

"Consider it pure joy, my brothers and sisters, whenever you face trials of many kinds, because you know that the testing of your faith produces perseverance. Let perseverance finish its work so that you may be mature and complete, not lacking anything" (James 1:2–4 NIV).

Chapter 2

Failure

New Mercy

When Abram was ninety-nine years old, the Lord appeared to him and said, "I am God Almighty; walk before me faithfully and be blameless. Then I will make my covenant between me and you and will greatly increase your numbers." Abram fell facedown, and God said to him, "As for me, this is my covenant with you: You will be the father of many nations. No longer will you be called Abram; your name will be Abraham, for I have made you a father of many nations. I will make you very fruitful; I will make nations of you, and kings will come from you. I will establish my covenant as an everlasting covenant between me and you and your descendants after you for the generations to come, to be your God and the God of your descendants after you. The whole land of Canaan, where you now reside as a foreigner, I will give as an everlasting possession to you and your descendants after you; and I will be their God." (Genesis 17:1–8 NIV)

Here we go again with great and wonderful promises from God. He has an insatiable desire to lavish His goodness on us. He is relentless, unstoppable. He just keeps putting forth great effort to bless us and make our name great.

When you read a promise like this one, how does it make you feel? Does it stir something inside of you to know that the God of the universe wants to do great things for you? Not only does He want to do great things for you, but He is able—*more* than able—to keep every promise He makes to you.

When I read this promise, I consider that Scripture says that God has a wonderful plan for me and wants me to have an abundant life filled with His goodness. I just want to say, "Wow!" I can only imagine what Abraham must have felt as God said these words to him. But there is so much more behind the promise.

Yes, God renewed His promise and reminded Abraham of the plans He had for him. And what if I told you that just before God said these words, Abraham made a horrible choice not to trust God, to take matters into his own hands, to become his own god. But following this incredibly arrogant sin, God renewed His covenant with Abraham. Though Abraham had sinned, God renewed His promise of great plans. On the heels of Abraham's sin, God did not close up shop or disappear. On the contrary, He stayed and held on tight to His plans for Abraham.

You see, after God promised Abram that he would have a son, Abram and Sarai got together and figured that it was impossible for her to have a baby in her old age. Rather than trusting God for a miracle and expecting something great from an almighty God, they decided that God was unable to accomplish what He had established and decided that they needed to help Him.

Have you ever attempted to help God?

We may think we're helping God when we start to move in the direction we think He wants us to move, but we do it in a way that He would not approve of. This is the situation with the man who is called to preach but who wants to start preaching without studying and showing himself approved. This is situation with the businesswoman who believes that God wants to bless her business, but to help Him along, she cuts some corners and does a few unethical things here and there, all the while calling upon the Lord.

Here is a revelation for all of us, including me: God doesn't need our help! God has designed His work so that we are partners with Him in this great journey of life, but it is not because He needs us. He allows us to partner with Him so that, through the process, He can teach us by pointing out where we have gone astray and praising us when we do well. He comforts us in our pain and strengthens us in our weakness. We are His partners on this journey, because this is how He teaches us, but He does not need our help. He can do whatever He wants, whenever He wants, however He wants. To be a good partner with God, we must follow His leading, do things His way, and stop trying to take shortcuts to blessings. There are no shortcuts on this journey with God. Each step is designed for teaching and maturing, preparing you for the greatest days of your life. Stop trying to help God. Trust me. He's got it under control!

Of course, we have all tried to speed up the process by moving too quickly. I know I have.

Saul did not want to wait for Samuel, so he offered the sacrifice that only Samuel was authorized to offer. He tried to justify it, but God was not pleased, and that was another step closer to the end of Saul's reign over Israel. Saul was worshipping the Lord, but there was rebellion and arrogance in the worship. God will not honor sin, even if the intent of the sin is to serve God or to accomplish something good. That is a perversion straight from the pits of hell.

Trying to help God, Abraham took Hagar, his wife's servant, into his bed, with Sarai's approval. To be fair, this was not something unusual in those days when a woman was barren. Sarai was old, and she and Abraham had never had a child. When God promised to give them a child, they took matters into their own hands. By taking Hagar into his bed, Abraham was participating in something that did not require the supernatural power of God to accomplish the promise. There was nothing spectacular about this process. There was no miracle. It was an act that did not require faith or anticipate the supernatural, even though the promise was from a supernatural God. They tried to help God.

Nevertheless, I want you to see God's response to Abraham and Sarai. He did not pronounce judgment, though He could have. He did not punish them, though He could have. He did not lecture them for hours upon hours for what they had done, though He could have. That's probably what I would have done if I were God. But in an act of unsurpassed grace, God just moved forward, renewing His plans for Abraham and Sarai. The Bible says that God's mercy is new each and every day. Each and every day. Did you hear that? Today, when you woke up, God was ready to forgive you and move beyond whatever happened yesterday.

I am not suggesting that there are no consequences for our choices. Abraham definitely saw strife within his own household as a result of what he had done. I am not saying that God just ignores our actions and prevents any ramifications. It was David who prayed, after his affair with Bathsheba, "Do not take your Holy Spirit from me." And we know that God will remove Himself in the face of continual sin, as the first chapter of Romans teaches. But we have to change our perception of God. He is slow to anger, and He abounds in love. Praise God!

If you are playing games with God, He will not be mocked. There is no doubt about that. However, God knows our hearts, and He judges us by our actions in relation to our desire. We may have a desire to please Him, but we fail. Sometimes we fail big and often. But He knows our hearts. And if we have repentant hearts and we confess our sins, He is faithful to forgive us. Too many people have a mental picture of God being up there in heaven with a lightning bolt in hand, just waiting for us to mess up, and then—*wham*!

But this is an inaccurate portrayal of our God. Just look at the cross. Christ did not come to the cross because the world was living for Him. He did not offer his body up for mutilation and murder because we somehow deserved that kind of grace. He gave Himself out of His love, not our faithfulness. This is why the Scripture teaches us that even when we are faithless, He remains faithful (2 Timothy 2:13). Like a good father, He does not beat us senseless when we mess up.

Some of you reading this now have never known any other kind of father. You grew up with a very critical, angry father who was never pleased with you. This is not the Father of heaven! Our heavenly Father is the one who responded to the sin of the world by coming to die on the cross and take the punishment of that sin on his own back. Our heavenly Father is the one who responded to Abraham and Sarai's sin by reestablishing the journey, the promise, and the blessing.

You are no longer in bondage to your sin. It's no longer necessary to beat yourself up for your mistakes. The people who taught you to do this to yourself are not God. They do not live in righteousness. They have no power. They are wrong. Today, the Holy Spirit sets you free from their words, their fists, their anger, and their neglect. Look to your heavenly Father, who will answer every new sin you commit with new mercy. Repent and confess. Don't pretend it didn't happen. But after you have repented and confessed, know with certainty that you are forgiven, that the great plans He has for you have not gone anywhere.

When you stop beating yourself up for your mistakes, then, and only then, will you be able to take a step back and learn from the situation. Allow God to teach you, redirect you, and discipline you in a loving way that can only come from God. It is a merciful discipline that says, "You messed up. Here's why. Let's learn this lesson and move forward and never return to this place again." Praise the Lord! You are forgiven! You are free! And the plans He has for you are right here, even now. Rest in this assurance.

> "For I know the plans I have for you," declares the Lord, "plans to prosper you and not to harm you, plans to give you hope and a future. Then you will call on me and come and pray to me, and I will listen to you. You will seek me and find me when you seek me with all your heart. I will be found by you," declares the Lord, "and will bring you back from captivity. I will gather you from all the nations and places where I have banished you," declares the Lord, "and will bring you back to the place from which I carried you into exile." (Jeremiah 29:11–14 NIV)

The "Bad News" about God's Love

From a very young age, we are taught that God loves us. Even in the Sunday school classes and learning center classes here at our church, the first Scripture that we teach is 1 John 4:16, which says, "God is love." The idea of being loved is an overwhelming thought, and to be loved as God loves is more than our minds can comprehend.

We have been designed to crave love, and we spend most of our lives trying to find it. For some of us, love is elusive, and we spend all of our energy seeking it. Because it is elusive, we are not always aware of what love is. We look for what we think love is, but too often our definition of love is incomplete or completely estranged from true love. This is when we find ourselves in abusive and destructive relationships. We find out that the words "I love you" can be empty and meaningless when not backed by action and behavior. When we hear about this God who loves us unconditionally and who backed it up with His actions on the cross—and that He will never stop loving us—we can be overwhelmed. But I want to caution you that there is both good and bad news in this love that God has for you.

The good news is that it is true: He loves you! He loves you without hesitation and without prequalification. You don't have to be anything for God to love you. He created you out of the overflow of His love, for the purpose of sharing His love with you. He has loved you since before you were ever born. His love has no qualifications. People in our lives may have said that they love us no matter what, but the truth is that we have felt their lack of love when we did not do things right or we weren't pretty enough or good enough.

But God loves you, just as He loved you when you rested in His hands before the day you were placed into your mother's womb. He loves you. There is nothing you did to make Him love you, so there is nothing you can do to make Him stop loving you. He is the lover of your soul, and His love never ends. If you don't get anything else out of this book, get this: you are loved, unconditionally and unequivocally. And this is the good news of God's love.

Now, here is the bad news: His love never stops. What? Does that sound right? This is ... *bad* news? How can a never-ending love from an almighty God be bad news?

Well, okay, maybe it is not bad news, but the foundation of His love is too great to sit back and watch us walk along unproductive and destructive paths. So His love prompts Him to move mountains and change hearts for us. There is nothing too small for Him to care about.

"Delight yourself in the Lord, and he will give you the desires of your heart" (Psalm 37:4 NIV). This is one of my favorite Scriptures. God not only supplies all of our needs according to His riches in glory, but He desires to be like the good dad who wants to give good things to His children—even beyond what we need and into the area of what we desire. I know, I know: it still sounds like good news.

Well, here it comes.

Because He loves you too much to let you settle for mediocrity in life, He will not just sit and do nothing when you are not following the way of blessing. He loves you too much. Therefore, He will close doors and force you to go to places that you do not recognize. He is leading you to true love. He is leading you to a love that never ends. He is moving you to the place where you are ready, willing, and able to receive His most perfect love.

Sometimes those doors slam hard in our faces. He will get our attention. If He can't get our attention through a still, small whisper, He will get our attention through a much louder and possibly more painful way. If that is what it takes to wake up our spirits, He loves us so much that He will let pain and suffering come our way to force us to our knees in prayer.

God loves you too much to let you be a loner. He loves you too much to just let you give up. He loves you too much to let you squander the plans He has for you. And in this love, He will force your hand. He will place you in a position where you have to either choose Him or reject Him. If you reject Him, He comes at you again. And every time you reject Him, the magnitude of the consequences increases, and life can become very difficult. He is trying to get you to turn a different way. This is love, nothing less. His love is relentless, even in ways that seem "bad."

Fight Him all you want. You can work hard to stay depressed, downhearted, and sad, but He loves you too much to let you stay that way. You can try as hard as you want to stay angry or bitter. You can expend all of your energies running after things that will only destroy you, but beware: The good news is the bad news. The love that loves you just as you are, loves you too much to leave you as you are. His love is always working to expand your dreams and fulfill your aspirations, but first He must turn your heart so that you are no longer attracted to things that destroy. He must turn your heart to the things that will be a blessing, not a curse. The bad news is the good news!

Undoing the Lies

"The Lord had said to Abram, 'Go from your country, your people and your father's household to the land I will show you. I will make you into a great nation, and I will bless you; I will make your name great, and you will be a blessing. I will bless those who bless you, and whoever curses you I will curse; and all peoples on earth will be blessed through you'" (Genesis 12:1–3 NIV).

Because God had great plans for Abram, He sent him on a journey. God's plan for your life will always involve a journey. It's the journey that gets to us. It's the journey that wearies us. It's the journey that causes us to grow impatient, frustrated, angry, bitter, depressed, and ready to give up. The plans that God has for us are wonderful. It's the journey that is difficult, but God's plans always involve a journey. You are on that journey even now, because His plans for you started before you were born. Even while you were in your mother's womb—in fact, even before that—God had plans for you. And because He had plans for you, you have been sent on a journey.

The plans that God reveals to us are designed to get us moving in the right direction on that journey. The journey is really what life is all about. God wants to give you good gifts, no doubt. He does want to bless you, certainly. But unless you are prepared for the blessings, the abundance of them will corrupt you. His blessings are so wonderful that it is possible for us to put our faith in them as if they were God. His blessings are so far beyond our imaginations that we can fall in love with them—more deeply than we love God Himself.

This is why the journey is essential. Unless we focus on the journey and purposefully set out to learn the lessons that come along the way, we will never see the full blessings that God has for us. We might see a snippet, but God's plan for us is abundant. Consider this Scripture: "The thief cometh not, but for to steal, and to kill, and to destroy: I am come that they might have life, and that they might have it more abundantly" (John 10:10 NIV).

God's plans are not small. They are not cheap. They are not insignificant. They are more than abundant. God is prepared to give you things of this world and of the spiritual world that are more than what your mind is able to imagine at this point. Even when we are greatly matured in our Christianity and we know that God's plans are beyond what we can imagine, we still cannot conceive of the most wonderful plans He has for us. The blessings are always increasing. The plan always involves more abundance. And since the plans of God never stop increasing, the journey on which God has set you never ends.

You are on this journey for life, so you'd better learn to focus on that journey. In fact, if you want to experience all that God has for you, the journey must become more important to you than the goal of the journey. If we focus too much on the blessings we hope for, we may get discouraged or quit because of how long it is taking. But in His great grace, there will be many blessings along the journey. Our goal and our focus must be the journey itself, more than the blessings along the many different stops.

"The heart is deceitful above all things and beyond cure. Who can understand it?" (Jeremiah 17:9 NIV). The heart is the seat of our emotions and our thoughts. The Bible interchanges the terms *heart* and *mind* throughout. The heart is the seat of my pain, joy, and desires—and the pattern of thinking produced by these. There is a lesson we must learn that is essential to our success on the journey. Very few ever learn this lesson, and few in this world teach this lesson. The lesson is this: what you think and feel can lie to you and deceive you more than the Devil himself, the Father of Lies.

My own emotions can lead me down the wrong road, even as they convince me that it is the right path for my life. I *feel* like I should do this or that. I *feel* like I am supposed to be with this person forever and ever, amen. I *feel* like I have a right to be angry. I *feel* like my life is over. I *feel* like I am better than everyone else. I *feel* like I am the worst person in the world and no one likes me. I *feel* like I will never succeed. I *feel* like I don't need anyone. I *feel* like I can't cope without someone to lean on. I feel … feel … feel. It never occurs to us that what we think and what we feel might be a lie straight from the pit of hell. Think back on how many paths you have taken in your life that were based on money, jobs, or relationships that seemed right and you *felt* good about—only to discover later that these were some of the biggest mistakes of your life.

The truth is that the Devil has been preparing lies for us since before we were born. He understands that if the parents and other significant people in a young girl's life teach her, whether directly or indirectly, that love is all about sex, then that young girl does not even realize that she is already in bondage to a lie. So many women have been taught that all of their value is wrapped up in how they look, and that the only way a man will stay with them and love them is if they give away their bodies. What a lie! So many men are taught that all of their value is wrapped up in how successful they become and how much money they can make, and that people will like them if they are wealthy. What a lie!

These lies did not begin when you turned sixteen or twenty-one. They started before you were born. They started generations earlier. The life perspectives of the most significant people around you, especially during your formative years, will lay down for you the workings of lies or the workings of truth. Jesus said that He himself is the truth. So only those who have the blessing of growing up among completely devoted Christians who are obedient to the core will have a foundation of truth. Their thinking will be influenced by the truth of God, not the lies of the Devil.

Be sure of this, though: I am not speaking of strongly "religious" people. Perhaps the most significant people in your life were very religious. But the Bible says that the spirit of "religion" brings death. Religion is all about rules and being perfect. No one will ever measure up to a religious

33

person's expectations. Religious people sometimes go to church, and sometimes they don't. They are mostly concerned with the rules that they believe constitute a right relationship with God.

Christ was clear in saying that none of the rules will ever disappear but that grace and love overshadow the rules. A strong foundation is laid by parents and people who live by grace and truth, not rules. They are mostly concerned that their children know they are loved.

Religious people are mostly concerned that their children are perfect. This focus on rules kills the spirit. It produces a young boys and girls who are weighed down their whole lives by trying to be perfect. They push themselves more and more to be better moms, dads, and business partners. They drive themselves to heart attacks, high blood pressure, volatile tempers, and impatience.

This notion that a person has to be perfect is just another lie, though it might be shrouded with religion and claims about God. It will kill the spirit. And when the spirit is dead, the flesh will rebel. This is when we see teenagers, who finally realize that they will never be perfect enough to earn the love of their parents, begin to act out in many different ways. When I talk about parents who are obedient to God to the core, I am talking about the God of the Bible, who teaches us that the greatest of all things is love, not rules.

So, let's take a moment and bash our parents. They did not know what they were doing. They were losers. How horrible they were!

Well, wait a minute. They were also victims of lies introduced before they were born. They learned what they were taught. They learned that love could include abusive behavior and still be love. They learned that love meant that Daddy could crawl into bed with you at night and touch you where you did not want to be touched. They learned that love meant being a workaholic. Lies, lies, lies!

But they learned these lies, and under those circumstances, they did the best they could. Bashing your parents will only take you down the wrong turn along this journey. They had their own battles, and they too were attacked, long before they were born. The Enemy has been working for many generations to destroy you. It did not start with your mom or grandmother or great-grandfather. It has been passed down for generations.

Of course, we are all responsible for our own actions. I do not want to give us a simple "out" by blaming others. We are responsible. The Scripture teaches us that He has made Himself known—outside of the influence we have received from people—through the creation of the world and the workings of nature. So there is no excuse. The magi who traveled from the East to see the baby Jesus did not have a Bible. They were not reading the Torah. They were not Jewish. God made himself known to them through a star.

For your entire life, God has been attempting to draw you to Himself for healing and for the correction of these lies. He wants to draw you outside the framework of deception that has been presented by the Enemy in your life. We are responsible for choosing to go to Him or not. The length of time it takes for us to finally turn to Him is completely and totally our responsibility. He has made Himself known, but the lies may have been so strong and powerful that we did not turn to Him right away.

We cannot compare ourselves to others. Not everyone begins in the same place. The woman raised by a drug-addicted prostitute is going to have a more difficult time finding God than the woman raised by a loving Christian mother who set out every day to put the needs of her daughter before her own. We don't start out in the same place, and therefore God does not deal with us all in the same way. His grace is sufficient for all of us, no matter where we might begin.

The purpose of the journey is to undo what's been done. It is to teach us what is true, compared to what we have believed to be true all of our lives. Along the journey, God will separate your emotions and lay out which ones you should feel and which ones you need to let go of. He will point out your reactions to past situations. He will show you the reasons you reacted the way you did, and He will teach you how those reactions must change in order to receive all that He has for you.

The journey is difficult. You are not traveling cross-country in the smoothest-riding Cadillac. No, this is more like a journey on a covered wagon with wooden wagon wheels across the roughest terrain. It is slow. It is rough. It is difficult. But the rewards are great.

After David had committed adultery with Bathsheba and had murdered her husband, he realized that there were some things he needed to learn and change about himself. In the fifty-first psalm, he asked God to teach him truth in the innermost place. Then, after asking for truth, he said some strange things that give us an idea that David understood this journey. He knew the rewards, but he also was familiar with the difficulties.

Iniquity is the sin connected to our emotions. It is our way of acting, reacting, thinking, dreaming, and feeling. It is anger. It is insecurity. It is jealousy. It is stress and worry. We don't choose any of these things, but they are born into us, because the Devil has been trying to destroy us for generations.

Listen to the journey David described for getting victory over iniquity, the lies born into us that keep us from God's blessings: "Surely I was sinful at birth, sinful from the time my mother conceived me. Yet you desired faithfulness even in the womb; you taught me wisdom in that secret place. Cleanse me with hyssop, and I will be clean; wash me, and I will be whiter than snow. Let me hear joy and gladness; let the bones you have crushed rejoice. Hide your face from my sins and blot out all my iniquity" (Psalm 51:5–9 NIV).

To be cleansed with hyssop was to put an acid-type substance onto a wound. It was painful. The word *wash* here means "to scour." Imagine taking a shower with a wire brush. That's how David was describing this journey. He said, "Let me hear joy and gladness." This is what we desire, the goal we seek.

But then he said, "Let the bones you have crushed rejoice." The rejoicing, the joy and gladness, and the wonderful plans of God will come on the other side of this journey, where God will tear you down in order to build you up. He will bring you low that He might then exalt you.

Do not give up on this journey. At times it will be the most difficult thing you could ever imagine, but at the same time, God is gracious, and He will bless you along the way. He will be sweet to you, though He breaks you. He will be endearing as you suffer. At times, the blessings will overshadow the difficulty of the journey. He is a good God, who never breaks a bruised reed. When you come through each segment of the journey, there will be blessing, joy, and wonder, as never before. Blessed be the name of the Lord!

"Come, let us return to the Lord. He has torn us to pieces but he will heal us; he has injured us but he will bind up our wounds. After two days he will revive us; on the third day he will restore us, that we may live in his presence. Let us acknowledge the Lord; let us press on to acknowledge him. As surely as the sun rises, he will appear; he will come to us like the winter rains, like the spring rains that water the earth" (Hosea 6:1–3 NIV).

Surviving the Drought

"Now there was a famine in the land, and Abram went down to Egypt to live there for awhile because the famine was severe. As he was about to enter Egypt, he said to his wife Sarai, 'I know what a beautiful woman you are. When the Egyptians see you, they will say, "This is his wife." Then they will kill me but will let you live. Say you are my sister, so that I will be treated well for your sake and my life will be spared because of you'" (Genesis 12:10–13 NIV).

After Abram set out on this journey ordained by God, the first stop was wonderful. God told him to look around and said that all of the land he could see would be given to him. God renewed His promises, and Abram had a great time of worship. He built an altar as a way of honoring the Lord and to commemorate this joyous occasion.

We really enjoy commemorating those wonderful times with God. We build altars using songs or Scriptures. They become reminders to us of the most wonderful experiences with God. This is why we can sing some songs without really sensing any movement of the Holy Spirit, while other songs nearly cause us to fall over from the strong presence of the Lord. This is because we have revisited the altars of the past and the memories of God's goodness and faithfulness. We never seem to build altars to commemorate the hard times when we feel as if God has abandoned us.

After God and Abram had a wonderful time of worship together, God brought a drought that forced Abram into Egypt so he could survive the drought. The weather comes at the hands of God, and He commands what He wants and what He doesn't want. Be certain that God brought this drought, sending Abram into a pressure cooker.

Abram was a stranger in a foreign land. He also had a beautiful wife. She was so beautiful that Abram knew that Pharaoh was going to want her for his own wife. Abram, fearing that Pharaoh would kill him in order to take his wife, told Sarai to lie and say that she was Abram's sister rather than his wife. Abram was dealing with a great amount of stress and fear, and it was God who had sent him there.

Sometimes God will send you down to Egypt. It is part of the journey. He is revealing His journey to you or preparing you to perceive the plans He has for you, and sometimes you have to go *down* before you learn how to go *up*. This is not a thought that makes you want to shout hallelujah. It does not excite the soul to the point of being overjoyed. In fact, these places along the journey are very difficult. They are a type of famine where we lack love, understanding, forgiveness, and grace. Instead, there is an abundance of heat. The sun of anger, bitterness, failure, and jealousy burns down hard.

This is a place that we want to avoid. We pray, day after day, asking God not to let us go down to Egypt: *Lord, keep us in Canaan where the blessings are abundant and your presence is so evident. No, Lord, not Egypt. Don't send us down there!* But this is part of the journey. We can't avoid Egypt. Our journey must go through Egypt—probably many times—as God reveals His plans for us.

Going down to Egypt reveals our character. I can say all day that I am committed to the Lord and His ways, but it's in Egypt where I can really see how committed I am. Peter proclaimed in front of all of the other disciples, "Lord, I will follow you even unto death." That turned out to be much easier for Peter to say than to do. After the rooster crowed, how terrible he must have felt when his eyes met the eyes of the One he had denied knowing. He had said one thing in the safety of Christ's presence, but when the pressure was on, down in Egypt, his fear and unfaithfulness were revealed.

These pressure-cooker situations are unpleasant, but they are incredibly helpful if we will stop being so angry at being down in Egypt and try to see what comes out of our hearts and spirits. We must listen to our words and consider our actions when we are down in Egypt. It is to our advantage to see what is truly in our hearts, because the prophet Jeremiah reminded us that sometimes what we feel and think about ourselves can deceive us. Our prayer in Egypt must not be, "Lord, get me out of here." Instead, we must pray, "Lord, help me to be the person I want to be. Help me to have the character I have claimed to have. And reveal to me where I don't measure up, that I might work on that area of my life."

If we never learn who we really are, we will never get closer to God. You may be thinking, "No way, man. I don't want to go through Egypt!" But the presence of God in our lives is dependent upon our true faith, not our perceived faith. It is based on our true devotion, not our perceived devotion. It hinges on our true spirituality, not our perceived spirituality. What a tragedy for any of us to think that we are on a higher spiritual level of faith than we really are. We will continually wonder why God is not honoring the faith that we perceive we have. This way of life will produce bitterness.

We may think we are completely sold-out to the Lord Jesus Christ, and thus we expect that He will keep His promise to give us the desires of our hearts (Psalm 37:4), when all the while, we are not who we think we are. Only in Egypt are we able to see who we really are. In Egypt we learn where we are lacking in faith and strength. We also get to see where we have grown, as we compare this trip to Egypt to our last time there. Egypt is the barometer of truth that reveals to us our faith and strength. Only when we accept what is revealed in the "Egypts" of our lives can we begin to work on the areas that need work.

I don't think that the day Peter denied Christ ever left Peter's memory. I have committed sin like that. My mind can still revisit those occasions at any moment. In fact, even as I am typing on my laptop right now, I am very aware of sins I have committed that were very much like Peter's sin that day, if not worse.

But, like Peter, I imagine, the pain I feel in my heart from those memories challenges me to never go there again. I was not even aware that I *could* go there. Peter never would have dreamed that he would be capable of denying his Lord, but his perception was off. After it happened, Peter worked on that area of his life.

The Scripture teaches us to put forth effort in growing spiritually. We have to "work out" our salvation. Egypt tells us what exercises must be done in our spiritual gym. We learn what Scriptures we should be memorizing and meditating upon. We see where we need to establish some self-imposed boundaries to avoid temptation.

The end result of going down to Egypt—if we allow God to teach us—is spiritual growth. We can't have spiritual growth without going down to Egypt. We can't have spiritual growth if we are bitter and angry that God has let us go or has sent us into Egypt. Egypt is part of the journey. Pain is part of the journey. Betrayal is part of the journey. Disappointment and failure are part of the journey. You will go down to Egypt. It is unavoidable.

The key is in how you come out of Egypt. Will you come out determined to strengthen the areas that have been exposed as weak and anemic? I am not saying that Egypt is going to be fun, but the results of Egypt can be awesome and cause for celebration.

Are you down in Egypt today? It stinks. It's hot. You don't like it. I understand that, but if you maintain negative feelings about your Egypt, you will never learn the lessons of Egypt. Yes, at each destination, there are those who seem to work hard at messing up your dreams and making your life difficult, and you can claim to have good reason for your anger or bitterness. The problem is this: by remaining angry or continuing to grieve over what someone did or what God allowed to happen, you will keep your eyes and ears shut to the lessons God is teaching.

Just let the anger go. Forgive. Look forward, not backward. There is a reason you are in Egypt. This is part of the journey. God was preparing Abram for something greater, and He is preparing you for something wonderful. Be patient. Be thankful. If you don't go through Egypt, you will never get to where God's greatest plans for you are. There is a reason for all of this. He is preparing you for greater plans and gifts.

Just Passing Through

Abram did not do so well in Egypt. He let fear control him. He put himself first and sacrificed his wife's security, not caring how she might feel about her husband forfeiting her to another man just to save his own skin. The fear of death caused Abram to lose his faith. Egypt was a very difficult place for him, with hard lessons to be learned. God used these lessons to reveal to Abram a lot of places to work on.

Have you ever really messed up like that? It is a horrible feeling. There have been times in my life when I have done things that brought me much shame later. I have completely amazed myself at the level to which I will sink if I am not keeping my eyes on the Lord. And it's when I bow my head before God to pray that I am overwhelmed with guilt.

I confess to the Lord how horrible I feel that I have treated Him in this way. I tearfully cry out to the Lord, confessing to Him that I am aware of my spiritual depravity. I confess that without His presence each moment of the day, I easily slip into sinful thoughts, feelings, and attitudes. Then sometimes, as I am crying out, I am physically overwhelmed by the sense that I can only explain as the Holy Spirit of God loving me rather than condemning me. That is what God did for Abram, even though he had really messed up.

Let's look at what happened. God sent a warning to Pharaoh. Pharaoh and all of his family became ill because Pharaoh had taken Abram's wife. Somehow God revealed to Pharaoh that Sarai was Abram's wife. Pharaoh called Abram to him and chewed him out. He chastised him. The words were coming out of Pharaoh's lips, but the words were God's, reminding Abram of his sin. Pharaoh then gave Sarai back to Abram.

One of my favorite Scriptures describes how God restores to us what the locusts have eaten. It is written in the book of Joel. "I will repay you for the years the locusts have eaten—the great locust and the young locust, the other locusts and the locust swarm—my great army that I sent among you. You will have plenty to eat, until you are full, and you will praise the name of the Lord your God, who has worked wonders for you; never again will my people be shamed. Then you will know that I am in Israel, that I am the Lord your God, and that there is no other; never again will my people be shamed" (Joel 2:25–27 NIV).

This is a fantastic promise, but what preceded the promise seems crazy. Israel had behaved very, very badly. They had done some of the most horrendous things, right in God's face, despite all of the kindness and blessings He had bestowed upon them. When the Israelites left God and His protection, they fell under a curse of locusts that destroyed everything. When they repented and came back to God, how gracious He was!

He promised not only to forgive them and to restore their hope for the future. No, His promise went even further. He promised to give back to Israel the lost years of the curse so that they could recoup all the blessings they had previously forfeited. Wow! What an awesome God we have!

After Abram sinned, lost his faith, and trusted in his own wisdom instead of God's wisdom, God still protected him! God did what Abram could not do. He responded to Abram's rebellion and arrogance by protecting his wife—and the plans He had for Abram. It would have served Abram right if God had found another man to receive His blessings. But God protected Abram's future, even after he had really messed up. God is faithful to us, even when we are not faithful to Him (2 Timothy 2:13). But let me back up just a bit.

When Pharaoh took Sarai to be his own wife, he honored her "brother" by giving Abram lots of gifts. In those days, if a man wanted to take a woman as his wife, it was customary to give gifts to the man who had authority over her, whether it be her father or brother. So Pharaoh had showered Abram with all kinds of wealth. When Pharaoh figured out what had happened, he was so ready to get Abram out of his country and escape the curse of sickness upon his family that he did not even ask Abram to return the gifts he had given to him.

All Abram wanted was to please God. He had gone on this journey for the very purpose of pleasing God. Although he failed and had a moment of weakness, the Lord knew that his heart was right. So the Lord not only gave his wife back to him, but through Pharaoh, God blessed Abram with extraordinary wealth.

We have to remember that God planned for Abram to become a great nation. It is hard to become a nation without a child, and you can't have a child without a wife—except, of course, in the case of the Virgin Mary. And it is difficult to become a great nation when you have no wealth. However, God responded to Abram's sin by continuing to prepare him for these great plans. "So Abram went up from Egypt to the Negev, with his wife and everything he had, and Lot went with him. Abram had become very wealthy in livestock and in silver and gold" (Genesis 13:1–2 NIV).

If you are in Egypt, don't give up! If, like Abram—and, frankly, like me and everyone else in this world—you have messed up, don't give up! This is not going to cause God to throw away His plans for you. Though you may have messed up, God is able to keep His plans for you steady.

The key is to accept Egypt. Accept the heat of the sun, the dryness of the land, and the lack. Learn from these hardships in your life, and hold on to God. And if you fail, don't give up. Fight through your lack of faith, and regain it. Fight through your sin, and regain your peace through forgiveness. Fight through your disgust and disappointment, and regain your hope and joy for tomorrow. God will not even let your sin cause Him to lose hope in you. He never stops believing in you, no matter how weak you may be or how horrible the sin you commit. He still believes in you.

Repent where repentance is needed. Renew your mind where newness is needed. Work on the areas of weakness revealed in your Egypt, but never give up. Egypt is part of the journey, but for those who endure, it is not the place where the journey ends. The more you fight with God in Egypt because you are mad at Him for taking you through this godforsaken territory of your life, the longer you will stay in your godforsaken situation. Instead, trust the Lord. Don't give up. Learn.

You may be in Egypt now, and the famine may be difficult, but do not lose hope, for you are just passing through. When you depart this horrible time of your life, you will be more prepared than ever to walk into the great plans God has for you.

The Little Foxes

God sent Abram into a very difficult situation when He sent him "down" to Egypt. It was God who ordained the drought that sent Abram to Egypt to survive. But it was there that Abram would be pushed by his own fear and selfishness to lie about Sarai and sin against God. It is important to understand that this was an essential part of Abram's journey. This was an important part of Sarai's journey. God did not set them up for failure, but He did push them into their weakness that they might see their own spiritual poverty. They needed to know that they could not succeed on their own, and they needed to know the areas of faith they needed to work on.

So many times—and even just yesterday—someone has said to me, "I don't understand why God lets certain things happen. I was going about my life, and everything was just great, and then all of a sudden *this* happened." Most of us have a goal, whether expressed or repressed, to enjoy life. This is what we seek to do each and every day. We just want to have fun and enjoy time with our friends and family. We want everything to go smoothly. We want to wake up every morning and not even have bad breath. We want breakfast in bed. We want body massages every day for free. We seek to enjoy life.

What we don't understand is that there are some blessings that cannot be enjoyed by an immature spirit. Our spirit is corrupted by a sinful nature, and this corruption causes us to be spiritually bankrupt or immature. As we mature, God trusts us with greater blessings. Our immaturity prevents us from receiving a blessing so that we are not corrupted by that blessing. And since all of us have a corrupted spirit, God must do some refining in order to take us to a place of greater blessing where life is even more enjoyable.

The deeper blessings are only available when we live life with a deeper spiritual maturity. If we live life at surface level, the only blessings we will have are those at surface level. The church is full of Christians living at surface level. They don't understand that there is more to the grace of God, and they don't understand how to access this greater grace. Because they do not taste the greater goodness of God, they become dissatisfied and are easily drawn away by temptations.

"Anyone who lives on milk, being still an infant, is not acquainted with the teaching about righteousness. But solid food is for the mature, who by constant use have trained themselves to distinguish good from evil" (Hebrews 5:13–14 NIV).

If we never strive to live life at a deeper level, we will be easily deceived. We will be deceived by people, opportunities, and circumstances. We will find ourselves in situations that are very difficult and destructive, even though they might have looked good on the surface or appeared to be a potential blessing. Even if we know that something is not good for us, the fact that it appears good on the surface might give us reason to justify doing it—only to learn in the end that it is not nearly as rewarding as we once thought it was.

How many of us have started a job that looked good on the surface, and then found out later that our employer was unethical? So many people have married someone who seemed wonderful on the surface but who did not turn out to be wonderful. All of the destructive sin that we commit is a result of having thought that something bad looked good or justifiable on the surface. The Devil doesn't run around trying to get Christians to murder or commit adultery. He tempts them to hang on to anger and to justifying it because they are hurt. He gets a man to take a second, lustful look at a woman and to justify it by saying that it doesn't hurt anyone to just look. Maybe on the surface these things seem insignificant, but these "little" things are so very dangerous.

The Bible teaches us that it is the "little foxes" that ruin the vineyards (Song of Songs 2:15). Usually, we think that the *big* foxes are the ones that destroy the vineyard, just as we think that the big sins destroy our lives. Scriptural wisdom teaches us that there are a lot more little foxes, and when combined, they do far more damage. We face many "little" temptations in life, but we don't realize that they add up quickly and destroy us. We would never consider committing many of the big sins—unless our self-control is first watered down by the "little foxes."

A lack of spiritual maturity keeps us from clearly identifying the snares of the Enemy. We fall victim to the little foxes and never make it to the greater blessings. So maturity is a must, not only for greater blessings but also to avoid greater hardships and traps in this world. Too many Christians want to just stay put in their walk with God. They learn only so much, and that's it. They grow only so far spiritually, and then they stop going to church, stop studying the Bible on their own, or stop praying.

It is impossible to just sit still in our relationship with God. He commands us to continue to grow and mature in our understanding, knowledge, love, and obedience to Him. If we don't do this, we are being disobedient. We cannot grow when we are disobedient. He is teaching us that the greater blessings and accomplishment require spiritual maturity, and if we choose not to grow, then we are either rejecting His blessings or rejecting His call to do something great. Either way, we move backward in our walk. We must set out to grow and mature spiritually.

If we really believe this, the difficulties in this life will be worth the spiritual growth they spur in us. The times when God sends us "down to Egypt," as difficult as they may be, will be worth it. The lessons learned in Egypt will make it possible for us to grow further in our spiritual maturity with Christ.

God was teaching Abram trust—complete and total trust. Even this particular lesson would not be enough for Abram, and the whole episode would play itself out again. Be careful: if you refuse to learn a lesson that God is teaching, He will just keep teaching you, and it may not be pleasant. Abram would soon lie again about his wife, for the very same reasons as the first time. But through it all, God was teaching him that absolute trust and obedience are the key to life's journey.

We are not always able to discern good from evil, but we can always just obey. When in doubt about what is going on or what God might want you to do or say, just obey. I have spent years trying to teach my children to just obey. Maybe you don't understand or don't agree with what God is doing or not doing. Maybe you are confused about how you should move, react, or respond. My answer is simple: just obey. Sometimes you don't have to know the answer or understand the reason, because God is teaching you how to obey when you don't understand. How many women could have saved themselves so much trouble if they had just obeyed Proverbs 22:24 (NIV): "Do not make friends with a hot-tempered person, do not associate with one easily angered."

Just obey. This is the beauty of a relationship with God, if you ask me. We are so easily fearful and doubtful. If we were to see what we are going to face, we might shrink back and fall away. So God does not always show us everything, only the next step. That next step is usually found in obedience.

We may not know how to respond, but we know that we should never let anything out of our mouths except that which is good for building others up (Ephesians 4:29). I know. I have been there. It seems so right to respond to someone who is lashing out by lashing back at them. It even feels liberating to trade an insult for an insult. But this is a little fox. Try obeying Ephesians 4:29 during an argument, and see how it affects everything when compared to returning insult for insult. "Do not let any unwholesome talk come out of your mouths, but only what is helpful for building others up according to their needs, that it may benefit those who listen" (Ephesians 4:29 NIV).

The Scripture is full of this kind of stuff. If we will just obey, God will do the work of changing hearts, minds, and situations. He will move mountains for those who honor Him. If we grow and mature, we will suffer, no doubt, but isn't it worth it to be able to avoid the traps and snares of people with wrong motives? How much more enjoyable would life be if we just learned how to join ourselves to good and positive things in life and avoid people and circumstances that bring us down?

It really comes down to trust. You can trust Him. He is the Good Shepherd, who takes care of His sheep. He is the benevolent Father, who always wants something better for His children. He is love, and He will take care of you. Hold on to Him through the valleys, and He will surely bring you back to the mountaintops. God is good!

Maybe you have never really believed that He is good, but I want to challenge you to follow hard after God. Just try living this way, and see if God does not prove Himself. The Bible teaches us to taste and see that the Lord is good. If you have never given yourself fully to trusting (obeying) Him, just try it. Taste a bit of what life is like when you trust Him in all that you do, rather than trusting your own understanding or your own emotions.

Prepare yourself, as there will be suffering, but know that it will be followed by the greatest blessings and accomplishments. Your life will mean something. You will have purpose, and that will give you a joy that overflows with the glory of God.

Chapter 3

Preparing for Greater Things

Blessings Are Dangerous

We have been created by God to commune with Him. We are made in His image, and His breath gives us life. We have the presence of His Holy Spirit. God designed us this way, because His purpose for us was communion with Him through worship. This creates in us a natural desire to worship. However, the sinful nature within us—a result of Adam's sin in the garden of Eden—keeps us from naturally worshipping God.

The key to walking in the love and plan of God is greatly affected by what or whom we worship, because we *will* worship something. Even those who claim there is no God will worship something, though it may be a relationship, a career, or even just an idea. We can very easily start to worship things and people that do not deserve any kind of worship. God teaches us that He is a jealous God and does not want us to worship anyone or anything but Him. God is jealous, not in a sinful way but in a parental way. He knows that if you have any other god before Him, you will miss eternal life.

Some people will say, "How can a good and benevolent God throw someone into hell for all of eternity?" I suggest to you that the premise of this question is not logical. God is love, no doubt. But as He is full of love in its purest form, He is also not a respecter of persons. He does not love any person or race more than any other. He loves the white man as much as He loves the black man. He loves the poor man as much as the rich man. He loves the prostitute as much as He loves the nun. He loves the rapist as much as the victim. He loves the child as much as the adult, and the female as much as the male. He loves people like Hitler and Satan-worshippers as much as He loves Billy Graham and T. D. Jakes.

He is also a holy God. Holiness and love go together. Pure love does not allow God to love anyone more than anyone else. Holiness does not allow for God to let anyone into heaven unless they are perfect. Yes, I said it. In order to go to heaven, you must be perfect. This is due to the holiness of God. He cannot allow anything defiled into heaven, the dwelling place of His presence. Everything in heaven is perfect; otherwise the defiled thing allowed into heaven would bring with it sin, temptation, heartache, and stress.

But God has promised that heaven is a place of rest. We would never be able to rest in heaven if sin were present. So, to get through the gates of heaven, we must be perfect, without sin. The problem for God is that no one is perfect. The Bible says that all have fallen short of the glory of God. So how does this God—who is full of love and doesn't want anyone to go to hell, but who is also full of holiness, thereby preventing Him from letting imperfect people into heaven—fix this issue. Well, He becomes a man.

Jesus Christ, who is God, chose to come to earth and live His life as a human being. He lived in total dependence upon the Holy Spirit, not His own supernatural power. His powers were only used for other people, never Himself. As a man, He never sinned. He was tempted in every way, the Scripture teaches us. He was only tempted because He was living as a human being. Had Christ been living as God, He would not have been tempted by anything, but the Scripture says that, as a man, He was tempted.

However, Jesus never sinned. The Bible says that when God spiritually put all the sin of the world upon the shoulders of Jesus Christ, He *became* sin. Until that moment, He'd had no sin. He became our sin and took our punishment on the cross. His crucifixion was a legal death penalty by which one man took the punishment for the sins of the entire world.

Now, anyone who accepts this gift from God—Christ's taking our place on the cross—will have everlasting life. His sins are removed from his account and are given to Christ. A person's faith in Christ allows his account to be free from sin. In heaven, those who have accepted Christ, by faith, as their Lord and Savior will stand before God, being credited with the perfection of Christ, because He was credited with our sin. Without this substitution, we would all go to hell forever.

This was the only way to solve the dilemma that faced a holy God who did not want a single soul to spend eternity in hell. Christ had to be a man, because sin had entered the human race through a man. He had to undo what had been done in the garden of Eden. He had to be perfect. Had Christ ever sinned, the punishment He received on the cross would have been the due penalty for His *own* sin, making him ineligible to receive the punishment for the sins of the world.

Now, let me bring you back to where I started. God does not send anyone to hell. We all have been destined to hell because of our own sin. Sin entered the world through Adam, and since then, every human being—with one exception, Jesus Christ—has sinned against God. So, if we go to hell, we are sending ourselves there. God has given us a way to be free from our sin. When we put our faith in Jesus Christ as our God—and this is evident in the way we live our lives—an exchange is made. Our sin is given over to Him, and His perfection is given over to us, rendering us "perfect." Then we are eligible for heaven.

God is jealous, because He knows that anything we worship other than Him will keep us from this exchange, this substitution. He is jealous, but not because He is mean or ruthless. He is jealous for your soul, because He knows that faith in Him is the only way that the punishment for our sins can be satisfied, rescuing us from hell. And He does not want anyone—*anyone*—to go to hell. People will not end up in hell for all eternity because God forcibly threw them into hell. They will end up in hell forever because of their own choice to reject the gift of Christ's sacrifice for their sins.

As humans, our propensity to worship anything that seems good, combined with God's incredible generosity, makes the idea of blessings very dangerous. For a moment, let's consider the Israelites as they left Egypt. When Moses led them out of Egypt, where they had been enslaved for four hundred years, they were going to be united with Jehovah, their God. God knew that He wanted them to build a temple, and He wanted the temple to be built out of gold to symbolize His purity and holiness. But how could they? They were Israelite slaves. They had nothing. They were dirt poor.

So God turned the hearts of the Egyptians toward the Israelites. God told his people to ask the Egyptians for their wealth as they were walking out of Egypt; and the Egyptians gave it to them. The Israelites went out into the desert with so much gold that they had to heap some of it onto the shoulders of their children. What a blessing! They went from being a poor, enslaved nation to possibly the wealthiest nation in the world at that time, for we know from history that Egypt was extremely wealthy at that time. What a blessing! God is so good! Right?

When they got out of Egypt, God called Moses up onto the mountain in order to receive the law, including the Ten Commandments. While waiting, the people became restless. They forgot about Moses and God and began to worship the blessing. When Moses came down, he asked Aaron, whom he had left in charge, what had happened.

> He said to Aaron, "What did these people do to you, that you led them into such great sin?" "Do not be angry, my lord," Aaron answered. "You know how prone these people are to evil. They said to me, 'Make us gods who will go before us. As for this fellow Moses who brought us up out of Egypt, we don't know what has happened to him.' So I told them, 'Whoever has any gold jewelry, take it off.' Then they gave me the gold, and I threw it into the fire, and out came this calf!" (Exodus 32:21–24 NIV)

That is one of my favorite Scriptures, not because it is nice and sweet but because it reminds us how quickly we can turn from God. Aaron told Moses, "We threw in the gold, and out popped this golden calf." The people began to engage in all kinds of horrible behavior as religious worship of this golden calf. Their blessings had been used to create a false god. Their blessings had made it easier for them to rebel against God.

God must be careful with us, because our blessings can become our downfall. If God blesses us with promotions and more money, this blessing will enable us to indulge ourselves in bad behavior as much as it allows us to pay the bills or give to the church. If God were to give us a great and wonderful spouse, we might be tempted to trust in our spouse more than our God. If He gives us a great church, we might be tempted to spend all of our time with people from the church and never go out to the lost souls of the world.

God wants to give us so many blessings in our lives that we can't even contain them. The Bible says that they are more than we could ever imagine. The blessings that God has for us, the plans that He has designed for us, are so wonderful that they are dangerous. At any moment, we could start worshipping our blessings. So this journey we are on is about refining our hearts and purifying our motives so that when God drops these wonderful things into our lives we will not worship our blessings more than Him. I know that we all want life to be wonderful all of the time. I would love to eat Blue Bell ice cream at every meal and never gain a pound. In order to give us His most wonderful gifts and blessings, God must refine us, and that is what the journey is all about.

If we miss the purpose of the journey, life will be very confusing. The minute we start to believe that God's plans for our lives consist of His blessings alone, we will be lost in the wilderness. The Devil is all about counterfeit blessings.

Let's consider money for a moment. "To the man who pleases him, God gives wisdom, knowledge and happiness, but to the sinner he gives the task of gathering and storing up wealth to hand it over to the one who pleases God. This too is meaningless, a chasing after the wind" (Ecclesiastes 2:26 NIV).

In this passage of Scripture, wealth is handled by both the sinner and the man who pleases God. When the sinner has the wealth, he might be fooled into thinking that He is in God's will and is enjoying God's grace. On the other hand, while the man who pleases God has no money, he might be fooled into thinking that God is unhappy with him because he struggles financially.

But neither of these is true. Things that seem like blessings are not always blessings. We must not fall into the trap of judging our relationship with God by what seem to be blessings. Trust me, the Devil would make us all billionaires if he knew we would only use the money for our own destruction by feeding our vices, becoming arrogant, and trusting our money instead of God. The Devil really doesn't care if you leave this earth having gained what seem like blessings. He only wants to keep you from heaven.

Sometimes the most blessed seasons of our lives are those in which we have no earthly blessing to lean on. When all we have is God, we will turn to Him. Blessings are dangerous, and God is careful not to give us too much too quickly.

Are you seeking God—or the things He can do for you? We must seek Him and Him alone and let the blessings, or the lack thereof, fall where they may.

Refined

> But who can endure the day of his coming? Who can stand when he appears? For he will be like a refiner's fire or a launderer's soap. He will sit as a refiner and purifier of silver; he will purify the Levites and refine them like gold and silver. Then the Lord will have men who will bring offerings in righteousness, and the offerings of Judah and Jerusalem will be acceptable to the Lord, as in days gone by, as in former years. (Malachi 3:2–4 NIV)

As a society, we really don't fully understand this passage and what it means to us. Let me take just a second to explain the process of purification, especially before we had all of the technology that we have now.

A purifier, or refiner, would sit and hold a ladle of impure gold or silver over a fire. If he allowed the ladle to get too close to the fire, the gold or silver would be burned up. If he was not close enough, the impurities would not be burned out. So the refiner continually adjusted the distance between the impure silver or gold and the fire that would purify it.

Scripture teaches that this is what God does with us. He holds us in His hand, keeping us close enough to the fire—the problems, the issues, the trials and tribulations in life—to burn out the impurities of our souls. It is when we go through the worst times of our lives that we must choose whether or not we have faith in God. We can pretend all day long that we have faith—until we are forced into a corner where we encounter the fire of God.

It is in this fire that we make a decision to put our faith in God, and we pray, seek His face, and call upon His name as we look to Him for help. In this fire, we are forced to grow our grace, mercy, and love. In this fire, our forgiveness is forced to stretch further than it ever has. Our faith must push beyond its current boundaries in our hearts, lest it die. The fires in our lives push out everything that is not of God—as long as we are holding on to God.

However, at the same time, the refiner is making sure that we are not so close to the fire that we are destroyed. There is a mercy in the process, giving us a break from time to time. He blesses us to relieve the pressure. He prepares before us a table in the midst of our enemies (Psalm 23). He removes us from the fires of life, because He knows that if we are pushed too far, we will be burned up and destroyed. We will collapse from the pressure. We will give up out of frustration. We will quit.

He is an expert refiner. He knows how to read the fire and how to protect the gold. We can have confidence, even from within the fires of life, that God is purifying us so that we might be able to receive more blessings later. We will not be destroyed by the fires of life if we hold on to Him. Sometimes it will feel as if we are being destroyed, and no one likes to get too close to the fire. But even in those times—or maybe *especially* in those times—we need to remember that we are in the hands of God. Though the fires rage, He will not let us be destroyed. In His time, He will give victory and rest.

Blessings are dangerous. Without a pure heart, blessings transform into curses. The purification process is necessary to receive all the blessings. Because God's plan for our life is so grand, this purifying process will never end. There is never a point in our lives where we will reach a spiritual maturity that no longer requires purification. This life is full of the fire of God, but we are being perfected in it, not consumed by it! Praise God!

"I have said these things to you, that in me you may have peace. In the world you will have tribulation. But take heart; I have overcome the world" (John 16:33 NIV).

We must understand this process so that we are not discouraged when we are in the fire. The fire indicates the working of God, not the absence of God. All believers will have fire.

One of the greatest prophets of the Old Testament had to be Elijah. Elijah had the faith and anointing to call down a drought for the entire nation of Israel. By the favor of God, Elijah performed a miracle every day by increasing the oil and flour for the widow who was willing to help him. He also raised this same widow's son from the dead. Elijah's anointing enabled him to do miracles, and it culminated at the showdown of the ages: Elijah versus all the prophets of Baal, in front of the entire nation of Israel (1 Kings 18).

The nation had turned to the ways of their foreign queen, Jezebel. King Ahab did more evil in the sight of God than all the kings before him. God had sent Elijah to set things straight and call the nation of Israel back to the Lord. The showdown was intended to demonstrate whose god was really God. Whichever god rained fire down on the altar of sacrifice would be proven to be the true God.

The prophets of Baal called upon Baal, but nothing happened. Elijah prayed a simple prayer, and the heavens released a strong fire to consume the prepared sacrifice. The entire nation began to shout, "The Lord is God!" All the prophets of Baal were taken down into the valley and destroyed. It was a great victory, except for one thing. Ahab, the King, and Jezebel, the Queen, were spared by God.

It was strange: the nation turned back to God and the false prophets were destroyed, but God allowed the ringleaders to remain in power. God would eventually take care of them, but not yet. Jezebel sent a message to Elijah, letting him know that she intended to kill him. The fire from heaven and the conversion of the people was a great victory, but it was not complete. God proved that He was God, but He let the wicked live.

Elijah did not know how to handle this. Have you ever been in a place where you don't understand what God is doing or not doing? This is the fire. Notice that even this great man of God was challenged. This entire incident was not just about the nation of Israel; it was also a personal issue between God and Elijah. God was redeeming His people, *and* He was purifying His servant—all at the same time. Read the words of Elijah as he was brought close to the fire by what God had done.

> But he himself went a day's journey into the wilderness and came and sat down under a broom tree. And he asked that he might die, saying, "It is enough; now, O Lord, take away my life, for I am no better than my fathers." And he lay down and slept under a broom tree. And behold, an angel touched him and said to him, "Arise and eat." And he looked, and behold, there was at his head a cake baked on hot stones and a jar of water. And he ate and drank and lay down again. And the angel of the Lord came again a second time and touched him and said, "Arise and eat, for the journey is too great for you." And he arose and ate and drank, and went in the strength of that food forty days and forty nights to Horeb, the mount of God. (1 Kings 19:4–8 NIV)

God moved Elijah a little closer to the fire, because the process of purification never ends. The situation was difficult for this man of God. He just wanted to die. He did not want to continue. He said to God, "Take my life." He felt worthless, like a failure. "I am no better than my fathers," he said. God was teaching him that his journey was not about this victory. It was about being purified and moving ever closer to God.

God had left Ahab and Jezebel alive to stretch Elijah's faith and love. Could Elijah continue to be faithful to the Lord, even in his disappointment? Could he remain faithful during failure?

The process of purification is an ebb and flow of blessings and hardships as we are moved closer and further from the fire. God is not our genie in a bottle. He is not our sugar daddy, waiting to fulfill our wishes whenever we call upon Him. He loves us and desires a relationship. The purification process removes the junk in us that keeps us from that intimacy with God, and we all go through the fire.

But notice the sweetness of God as Elijah struggled to endure the fire. Elijah called for God to take his life. He was ready to quit. He had lost all faith. How did God respond to this lack of faith and quitter's attitude? He sent an angel.

I love that. (Thank you, God!) When we struggle in the fire, God does not condemn us. Instead, He sends help. The angel did not show up with the dry, crunchy manna of the desert. God responded to Elijah's bad attitude with hot bread. I like to think that if this had happened in our day, God would have sent an angel with chicken fried steak, cream gravy, mashed potatoes, steaming hot green beans, and apple pie à la mode for dessert. God was gracious, giving, and exceedingly kind. If you are struggling in your fire, hold on, because God will be gracious to you. He will send help. You will not die. You will not be defeated. The wicked will not win. Wake up and eat, for God has not forgotten you!

I am also blown away that after the first meal, Elijah went back to sleep, and God was okay with that. He understands our fatigue. He knows the weariness of trouble and pain. Again, there was no condemnation, but instead, there was a second course. The first meal was for healing the past. The second meal was to give strength for the journey. (While putting these words to paper, I had to stop typing to raise my hands in praise. What a gracious God we have! Thank you, Jesus!) This meal gave Elijah supernatural strength to make it all the way to the mountain of God.

Maybe today you are in the desert, wishing you were dead. Rest. The angels are on their way. You will get up, and God will bring you to Himself.

You are not being destroyed. You are being refined, prepared for greater things and a deeper relationship with God. The refiner knows that the gold or silver is pure when He is able to look at the gold or silver in the spoon and see His own reflection. Then He knows it is pure. He is trying to purify us, just as He is pure. In the Scriptures, God says, "Be holy, therefore, as I am holy" and "Be perfect, therefore, as I am perfect." He is purifying us.

It is not a fun process to be in the fires of life, but the more we are purified, the more we will be able to receive the greater blessings without being corrupted. We must never forget that even though He sets us in the fires from time to time, the purpose is to bless us so abundantly that it is noticed by others. Then, when they wonder how our lives are so blessed, we are able to say, "It is from the Lord Jesus Christ, and He is good!"

Of Greater Worth Than Gold

Murder. Rape. Porn. Adultery. Violence. Fornication. False religions. When we consider the idea of temptation and bondage to sin, we tend to think about all of the worst in things we can imagine in this life. We think of what we consider "evil" things. It is easy to see someone in bondage to pornography or heroine. But anything—*anything*, even things we might consider "good"—can become a temptation and sin that enslaves our soul.

In His teachings, Christ suggested that even our own families could be a temptation. The apostle Paul warned about marriage, because married people might worry more about pleasing their spouses than about pleasing God. Yet the Bible says that marriage is a good thing. So, is marriage a good thing or a bad thing? Obviously, it is intended to be a good thing, but even something good can become too important to us. It is spiritually dangerous to put even good things ahead of Christ. Good things, blessings, can be used by the Enemy to move our eyes just a little bit off of God, and with time, these good things can pull us far from God. Blessings are dangerous.

Even as you are reading this book, is it possible that some of the things God intended as a blessing have enslaved you? Some people may be enslaved to a husband or wife, worrying more about what that spouse thinks of them than they do about what God thinks of them. Perhaps in times of trouble you run to your spouse before running to God. Perhaps you look more to your spouse than to God for direction in life. This can cause you to move God off the throne of your life and replace Him with your spouse. Perhaps, you have even laid down the dreams God has given you for your life because of how your spouse might feel about them. You may not be tithing or going to church because of your spouse. It is easy to abandon what you believe God wants you to do in order to avoid a fight.

Some of you may be chained to your job. It might have been a good job at one time—or it might still be a good job—except that now your employer requires more of your time, and you are allowing the stress of the job to affect the way you act at home. It was a blessing when you got the job, but now it is your master, controlling your time, your mood, and your vision.

Can we receive any greater blessing than the children God gives us? For me, one of the greatest revelations of God is the perfection of a newborn baby. Yet these great blessings can enslave us. We might begin to obey a child's every desire to the point of not living to please God. They can cause frustration and stress that keeps us from being who we need to be spiritually. Many times we try to bless our children so much that we do not help them develop a solid foundation in church, because we are constantly doing so many other things with them and for them.

Do I dare even talk about money? The Bible says that God confirms His covenant with us by giving us the ability to produce wealth (Deuteronomy 8:18). Anything good that we want to do in this life takes money. God has given us the ability to produce wealth, and that wealth allows us to provide for our families, keep our churches open, and help the needy. The same money that can be such a blessing is also a temptation. "For the love of money is a root of all kinds of evil. Some people, eager for money, have wandered from the faith and pierced themselves with many griefs" (1 Timothy 6:10 NIV).

All I am trying to say is that, with every level of blessing, there is a greater temptation to allow that blessing to rule your life instead of letting God rule it. By all means, do not get rid of these blessings. But understand that God is using the blessing to bring to light what is in your heart. He is not doing this for Himself. He already knows what is in your heart. He has blessed you in this way to allow you to see what is in your own heart.

If you will take the time to be honest with yourself, you will see that these blessings have revealed that you are not as patient as you should be. You do not love as well as you thought you did. Perhaps you are more selfish than you realized. You may not trust the Lord with your money as much as you thought you did. With each greater blessing, God will give you a greater revelation of yourself. This is so you that you might then turn to the Holy Spirit and allow Him to burn away anything in you that is displeasing to God. This is a continual process throughout our lives.

This brings to mind a very good friend of mine, Vernon Winans. I would say that he was not only a good friend but a mentor in many ways. We met weekly at Marie Callender's, where he always ordered the same meal, followed by the purchase of an entire blueberry cream pie. We would each eat a slice, and then he would send the rest home with me for my family. We talked about spiritual things, deep things of life and of God. I cherish those moments and miss him now, even as I write these words.

I remember him as a spiritual giant. He was a prayer warrior, a saint of God. However, when he got sick and was on his deathbed, he realized that he was afraid and full of fear. He told me that God was challenging him to lay down his fear of death. He had always thought that he wouldn't be afraid of death, because he knew that he was headed to heaven. But he was afraid of the process, the pain, the suffering. Even on his deathbed, God was perfecting my friend's faith.

My first response might have been to cry out to God and ask why He would do this to someone so honorable on his deathbed. Why couldn't God just let him die peacefully? I later realized that God was challenging Vernon—but not just for Vernon. His experience was making an impression on me as I watched him wrestle with his fear and hold on to his faith. It actually gave me some fortitude and strength that I used later in my life to fight through my own doubts. In fact, when in doubt, I still think of Vernon fighting through this wrestling match.

God is refining each of us, and He does it before the eyes of others—our friends, family, church members, coworkers, and so on. As He refines and purifies us, we are made eligible for greater blessings. The purification process goes far beyond avoiding the "evil" vices of our world. It moves into the area of choosing God, "even the good things of life and the excellent things in life."

Consider the teaching of Christ: "If anyone comes to me and does not hate his father and mother, his wife and children, his brothers and sisters—yes, even his own life—he cannot be my disciple" (Luke 14:26 NIV).

Jesus has a way of making us sit up and take notice because of the strong language He uses at times. We know from the entire context of Scripture that God does not want us to hate anyone, especially our own family. His point is that our love for Him must far outweigh our love for family—even though He gave us those families, which are usually a great blessing.

Our ability to receive greater blessings without being corrupted by them increases. As His blessings increase, He receives more glory, as those who see us wrestle and gain victory in our faith will be inspired to also turn their eyes toward God. Whatever is enslaving you today, don't let it continue. Make a decision today to be set free from its hold, and then work toward remaining free. This is true even of blessings from God. Learn to receive them without worry or stress or temptation. The blessing illuminates the places in your heart that need to be refined, the places where we must confess to the Lord and receive from Him the power to keep Him first.

"These have come so that your faith—of greater worth than gold, which perishes even though refined by fire—may be proved genuine and may result in praise, glory and honor when Jesus Christ is revealed" (1 Peter 1:7 NIV).

There are very few blessings from God that do not present us with challenges. People become jealous. We worry, trying not to lose what God gave us. What a blessing Abraham received because God chose Him! And yet that blessing presented huge challenges. Many times, blessings are intended to give us influence with others. Our blessings draw the attention of others so that we might shine the light of Christ into their lives. This means that blessings by nature necessitate spiritual growth and responsibility. Because each blessing we receive from God is better than the last, we must work harder to not be so enamored or obsessed by the blessing, lest we forget God.

Our journey in this life is not about the blessings, nor is it about the curses. It is about our faith being refined. Like gold, our optimum state is purity. Any imperfections in our hearts keep us from the next great thing God has for us.

"And without faith it is impossible to please God, because anyone who comes to him must believe that he exists and that he rewards those who earnestly seek him" (Hebrews 11:6 NIV).

Did you read that? We must. We *must*. We *must* believe that God rewards (blesses) those who earnestly seek Him. This is not an option. If we are to come to God, we must believe this simple truth. The more God blesses us, the more we must work to force our affections toward God and not toward the blessings. It takes effort not to worship or remain more faithful to our blessings than to God. When we more earnestly seek Him, He rewards us. When He rewards us, we must seek Him more—to avoid the temptation to love the reward more than God.

So, we seek and He rewards. This process moves us to overcome anything and everything of this world. Our faith is solidified and purified more each time, allowing us to receive more and more without corruption. It is a beautiful cycle. Throughout this cycle, God will sometimes take us through a season without blessing—to see how hard we seek after Him instead of seeking what He can do for us. Through it all, He is preparing us for greater blessings, whether it be a better job or a higher level of patience and love.

This is His process, not just because He loves you, but because He is moving you from bondage to blessings right before the eyes of others. He is seeking to save, and the blessings are a visual aid that people can see in us, giving evidence of a God they can't see. Our journey is continually preparing us to be more blessed and thus to be more visible to a dying world.

Please don't think that blessings are always tangible things. A blessing could be answered prayer. It could be wisdom. It could be a peace that doesn't make sense to people who do not know God. These intangibles are greater blessings.

Keep seeking Him and never let anything in this world become more important than God Himself, not even the blessings that come from His hand. Let the Holy Spirit progressively bring more purity to your heart, your mind, your dreams, and your vision. He is refining your faith that you might be a great light with great influence to draw people to the saving grace of Jesus Christ. Just as pure gold is more desirable than gold with impurities, so the world needs to see your refined faith. This purity will cause your life to have meaning and purpose. You will be used by God in ways you never imagined. You will see miracles in others' lives because of how God uses you on this journey. Your life will make a difference.

God is refining your faith, and this will lead to blessings, praise, and exuberance. Praise His name!

Finishing Strong

Our journey with God is what we make of it. Sometimes we look at different people and think to ourselves that God loves them more or that God has a better life planned out for them. However, God is not a respecter of persons. While it is true that we do not all start out in the same position, God's desire to bless us is the same for everyone. He wants to bless Billy Graham as much as He wants to bless the people who planned the 9/11 attack that killed so many Americans. He wants to bless the church-going, always-praying, humble-in-heart Christian as much as the worst serial killer or rapist.

This is difficult for us to get our heads around, but it is true. God does not look at you and compare you with the rest of the world and then decide how much of a blessed life you deserve. His love and plans are the same for every human being, though very few will ever allow themselves to be in a position to receive these great plans from God.

I did say that we do not all start out in the same place. Another difficult concept about God is that He allows sin to pass down through families for generations. Sin passes down within cities and nations and even local churches. When there is sin in these arenas, the sin is passed down, and people who had nothing to do with the sin of the past are punished. It seems harsh, I know, but consider this passage: "But women will be saved through childbearing—if they continue in faith, love and holiness with propriety" (1 Timothy 2:15 NIV).

This is such a strange statement. A woman will be saved through childbearing. We know that salvation is spiritual. It is the result of a person's decision to follow Jesus Christ as Lord and Savior by faith. How does giving birth bring about this kind of decision in a woman? Well, it doesn't mean that all women who have ever given birth will be Christians. So what does this Scripture teach?

We learn from this passage that God uses our children as a way of moving our hearts. He desires that the love of men and women for their children will move the parents to want the best for those children and to love them with all that they have. He hopes that when we see the results of our own sin falling upon our children through their behavior, their health, their self-image, and so on, we will be willing to change. He hopes that even if we don't love ourselves enough to get our own lives straight, perhaps our love for our children will motivate us to get our lives straight with God.

God works this way so that nations, cities, and churches all go through this. In different areas, we see suffering in our families, our cities, our nations, and our churches. God hopes to motivate us to cry out to Him and return to Him. We are now seeing in our nation a call to pray and a return to morality, because the population of believers in our country sees how the decline of morality is destroying our society. We can now see the effects of previous generations not standing strong in their Christian beliefs, and these consequences are motivating many people to call for a return to what we have lost.

People, churches, cities, and nations do not always begin on equal levels. One girl may be raised in a very healthy home with a loving father and mother who instill within her a love for God and a healthy love for self. At the same time, this girl's friend at school may be going through horrible abuse or molestation, developing sadness, bitterness, and anger, possibly in a single-parent home where she doesn't get much attention. Though God's desire for blessing both girls is the same, they do not start out the same.

Too often we mistake these uneven starting places as God playing favorites, but this is not true. God loves the parents as much as He loves the child. So He allows the child to suffer in the presence of his or her parents, hoping that the parents will turn to Him so He can save both the parents *and* the child. We are all His servants, and He sometimes allows us to suffer to put us in places where we reach people we might otherwise never see. Or sometimes He blesses us so that others can see the providence of God. In both cases, He is using us. This principle, however, should never be misunderstood as God loving one person more than another. He wants everyone to have the most blessed, abundant life.

We believe, for the most part, that God loves everyone. It's true that there are some who believe that God is just waiting to catch us messing up so He can strike us down to hell. But this is not God at all. Most people can say that God loves the whole world. We don't struggle with the idea of God loving the entire human race from a global point of view. Our struggle is found on a personal level. Somehow a person can believe that God loves everyone, and yet he wonders if that love applies to himself. I have counseled many people in my office who have no doubts whatsoever that God loves everyone, but they cannot find it within themselves to believe that God loves them personally. For some reason, we differentiate the two. But I want you to consider this incredibly powerful Scripture: "And without faith it is impossible to please God, because anyone who comes to him must believe that he exists and that he rewards those who earnestly seek him" (Hebrews 11:6 NIV).

Whoa! Did you catch that? If I am going to come to God—which means that I am going to be a believer, a Christian, and spend eternity in heaven—I *must* believe not only that He exists but that He rewards those who earnestly seek Him. God does not present this as an option. It is not something that I can kind of play with and see how I like it. It is simply the reality of salvation. If I am going to be a follower of Jesus Christ, I *must* believe that He rewards those who earnestly seek Him.

Oh, I know what you're thinking. You're thinking, *I don't always earnestly seek Him.* I understand that. I don't either. That is not the issue right now. The question is whether or not you believe that God rewards those who do. You see, if you believe that God only rewards those who are good, church-going, Bible-reading, passing-out-tracts, fish-on-the-back-of-the-car kind of people, then you believe that God rewards those who do certain things. The Scripture here does not specify what must be *done* except that we earnestly seek Him.

We tend to think that God rewards the "perfect" people. Well, here is a little secret: *there are no perfect people!* God rewards those who seek Him. Even the wording brings hope to my heart, because if I am having to seek Him, then I haven't completely found Him yet. This means I don't have all the answers. I don't do all the right things. I don't say all the right things. I can be earnestly seeking God and yet make many mistakes and even sin at times. I have to believe that the life of the apostle Paul would be described as one earnestly seeking God, and yet he wrote about his own wrestling with the flesh, doing things he knew were wrong, and wishing he could have done things right.

Do you believe that God rewards those who earnestly seek Him? If you believe this, then start seeking Him with sincerity and honesty. Make a an effort to get to know Him more and follow Him more radically. Then prepare yourself, because He will reward you. If you don't believe this, then you are probably thinking you are not good enough for His blessings.

To put it bluntly, I remind you that the Scripture says that you *must* believe this if you are going to follow Him. There is no choice. If you want to go to heaven when you leave this earth, you'd better start believing that He rewards those who earnestly seek Him. Make up your mind right now that you are going to believe this principle, regardless of anyone's past or current situation, regardless of their sin, regardless of … anything. Start seeking Him, and the blessings will come.

It's true that not everyone starts in the same place. Some people are born into very difficult situations. Some are born in countries where they never hear about Christ until they are adults. Some live very difficult lives, never knowing how to reconcile the idea of a loving God and a hellish life. This is the result of sin being passed down.

At the same time, there is no limit to what God can do in a person's life. Just because a person struggles early in life doesn't mean that abundant blessing is limited proportionately. Just because you get a slow start, it doesn't mean you have to lose the race.

In Scripture, there was a group of people known as the Samaritans. These were not full-blooded Jews, and there was racial tension between the Jews and Samaritans. Christ wanted to reach all of them. John 4 says that Jesus had to go through Samaria. He was preparing the way for revival in an area where people hated Jews. The social difficulties of moving the gospel into this area were immense.

When Jesus decided on His strategy to accomplish this task, He chose a woman. Women did not start out equal with men. Not only did Jesus choose a woman, but He chose a woman who had been shunned by the other women because of her sin and promiscuity. She had been married five times and was now living with a man who was not her husband. Even in our morally relaxed society, five marriages would be frowned upon, so can you imagine how much of an outcast this woman must have been.

But Jesus had a plan for her life. He chose this woman, and it was through her testimony that a revival began in the area. How it must have changed the way she saw herself—and even the way others saw her! We don't know much more about this woman. I have to believe that she made some pretty drastic changes in her life and began living a very blessed life. She may have started life behind others spiritually, but she finished very strong.

"The Lord had said to Abram, 'Leave your country, your people and your father's household and go to the land I will show you'" (Genesis 12:1 NIV). Even Abram was brought by God to a foreign country. Why couldn't God just bless Abram in his own country? He could have blessed him there and saved a lot of travel time. Instead, God purposely brought Abram out of the place where people knew him, where he had some kind of standing in the community. God took him to a foreign country, to a place where he didn't know anyone. He didn't have any land. He didn't have anything that would make it possible for him to succeed. God purposely moved him to a place where the odds were against him. Nothing was going to be easy.

God's journey for you will inevitably take you to a place where you are the underdog. He will bring you to circumstances that seem impossible to overcome. But then, like Abram, you will thrive. God makes us the underdog and then reveals His love and power by helping us overcome all obstacles and every hardship. This is part of the journey and part of His plan. David expressed it like this:

"The Lord is my shepherd, I shall not be in want. He makes me lie down in green pastures, he leads me beside quiet waters, he restores my soul. He guides me in paths of righteousness for his name's sake. Even though I walk through the valley of the shadow of death, I will fear no evil, for you are with me; your rod and your staff, they comfort me" (Psalm 23:1–4 NIV).

A path of righteousness is not an easy path. Righteousness only comes when we have been cleansed of unrighteousness. This happens through the refining process, which requires lots of heat near the fire. David spoke of a path of righteousness and then brought up the valley of the shadow of death. These are places for the underdogs of God. He brings us to these valleys and sets us up as underdogs. David said that God does this for His own name's sake. He must make Himself known, lest people die eternally, and He makes Himself known by taking His people through the valleys. Some of us start there, and others don't. In our journey with God, everyone called by His name—Christians—will be made underdogs so that when we overcome, God will be revealed.

Maybe you picked up this book because you felt that your life was in shambles, falling apart. You don't understand how God could let some of the things happen that you have experienced in life. Well, let me redirect your vision. You are looking at what you can see. God has called us to focus on what we *can't* see. Perhaps, what you have not yet seen will become clear right now.

If everything is broken and all odds are against you, you are in a prime position for abundance—if you earnestly seek Him. Though the Devil has been trying to destroy your future since before you were born, you can overcome. Your life is primed. You are ready to overcome. You *will* overcome. Your past does not limit your future. God's hands are open with blessing and greatness for His name's sake. He is going to do a new thing in your life. Seek Him earnestly.

Go for It

Hopefully, you have made up your mind to believe that God does reward those who seek Him. If this is the case, this may be a new experience for you—believing that something good is about to happen. Perhaps until now, based on your experiences in life, you have learned to live life waiting for the next horrible thing to happen. With a lack of faith in anything good, your relationship with God has been bittersweet at best. Maybe you've even tried to devote yourself to Him—or you've known that you should—but always, in the back of your mind, you've wondered how God could have let so many bad things happen.

Don't think for a minute that bad things are going to stop happening, because they won't. Never forget what Jesus said: in this world, we will have trouble. Then He went on to say, "I have told you these things, so that in me you may have peace. In this world you will have trouble. But take heart! I have overcome the world" (John 16:33 NIV).

You are still going to have troubles, but with your heart earnestly seeking God, and the faith that God rewards those who do, your outlook in times of trouble will be different. Though trouble comes, you can know that God is working on your behalf. He is going to use the hardest times of your life to produce in you a faith that can move mountains, and rest assured that those mountains will move. Prepare yourself for blessing. Expect blessing. Seek the Lord with all of your heart, soul, mind, and body, and then get ready for God to do a new thing in your life!

Because you have chosen to believe, you must now decide what you want your life to look like. There is a song by Switchfoot, and the lyrics go something like this: "This is your life. Who do you want to be?" It's your life, and you get to decide the kind of person you are. Let me stop you here very quickly, because this is not a motivational book about selling cars and creating the next iPhone so that you can be rich. This is about God's plan for your life. This is a plan that He reveals little-by-little. This is a plan that is always good, but it is also a plan that sometimes takes you through Egypt.

"'For I know the plans I have for you,' declares the Lord, 'plans to prosper you and not to harm you, plans to give you hope and a future'" (Jeremiah 29:11 NIV). This Scripture is not talking only about financial or career prosperity, but it certainly does include it. This word *prosper* is all-encompassing. His plan for you is to prosper in every possible way—in your health, your children, your peace, your love, and your relationships. Of all of these things, I would say that your career or bank account is the least important. However, financial and career success is still included as part of the word *prosper* and God's plan for your life.

Conversely, if we ever start seeking only one aspect of the word *prosper*, we are out of God's will. We should be seeking His prosperity in every part of our lives. This means that we don't have to sacrifice one to get the other.

When we get outside of God's will and start seeking after only one part of His prosperity for our lives, we will sacrifice another area. God's plan for you is to be different from the world. He wants to give you success in your career without your being a workaholic. You can have the best of all worlds. If the people you work for require workaholic hours, hold on, because God may change their hearts or He may open another door for you somewhere else. The point is that God's plan for you is better than what this world promises.

In case you haven't noticed, the world promises prosperity in only one place or the other—at work or at home. The world sends messages that we are to succeed, but we never see a message that says we can succeed both at work and at home. There are messages that tell us to be successful at work, and there are messages that tell us to be a better husband, but usually these messages aren't in the same commercial or ad. One force in the world encourages people to go after prosperity in their relationships. Another encourages people to go after prosperity in their careers.

But God is the only one who teaches that prosperity is possible in every area of our lives. He teaches us that it's not only possible, but it is His plan for us. "What no eye has seen, what no ear has heard, and what no human mind has conceived"—the things God has prepared for those who love him" (1 Corinthians 2:9 NIV).

Now that you have chosen to believe that God rewards not only the Billy Grahams of this world but anyone who seeks Him, the only thing left to do is to make up your mind that you want all the blessings God wants you to have. Don't settle for less in this life. Don't limit yourself. Don't limit God in what He can do for you. He is God. He is the master of the universe. He can do anything He wants at anytime for whomever He wants. He is not limited, and He cannot be stopped.

Hopefully, these Scriptures give an you an understanding that God wants to do so much for you and your life. He wants your life to be so abundant that it spills over into the lives of your friends and family as a witness of how good He is. This is His plan.

God's plan for you is prosperity in every area of your life, but it's not just about you. The purpose of His blessings on your life are for your benefit—and to reveal Himself to those who don't know Him. Blessings on believers are intended to make us stand out so that others take notice. Sometimes these blessings are the kind that make us smile. Other times they will be in the form of undying strength that allows us to overcome and thrive when the world gives up and dies.

So believe it. Live it. Go for all that God has. God talks about opening the floodgates of heaven and pouring out blessing upon us. Too many of us have settled for a few drops of rain or just the dew on the grass in the morning. He wants to flood you. He wants to *flood* you! His desire is to flood you with His goodness. Will you let it happen?

I want to encourage you right now to set this book down, commit to the Lord that You believe in His goodness, and promise Him that you are going to seek Him. Then ask Him to open the gates and release the floodwaters into your broken heart. May rivers of powerful waters run down the streets of your life so that your marriage rises to the top. May His goodness push over the obstacles at work and the sea walls of insecurity. My desire for you is that your life would be overrun with His goodness and blessing, so much so that everyone in your life is amazed at who you have become and all that God has done. I pray that this happens for you and for them. This is God's plan for your life.

The Hebrew word for *blessings* is a form of water—more specifically, a *pool*. Think about it. If we are going to consider the analogy the Spirit has given us in Scripture, then we must see that God does not just want to rain on us. He wants to flood our lives. It is awesome to think that this is what God wants to do for each of us. This is not just some kind of proverbial "carrot before the mule" to get us to do something. This is something that God wants to do for us. He is looking to flood us with His goodness.

He is not saying, "Well, I hope you get there, but it doesn't really matter to me." He is not the boss who has offered a bonus but offers little help to us in achieving the goal. God not only wants to do this for us, but He helps us along the way. God is saying that He is our Father, a Father who loves to give good things to His children. He is like the father on Christmas Eve, so excited about the gift he has for his children that he almost can't wait for the next morning. God wants to flood your life. It is His desire. The anticipation of watching you enjoy all that He wants to do for you is rushing through Him, and He almost can't stand it. He wants to bless you!

But back to the point. Let's suppose His blessings are rain. The word *blessing* is like a pool. If you are not deep, the waters are going to run off. If you want to enjoy the blessings, you must become like a pool. The deeper you are, the greater the blessings you can hold.

Too many of us are not enjoying the plans that God has for us, because we are too shallow. We have never gotten into the deeper truths of Scripture. Our commitment to the Lord is too shallow. I am not saying that we don't believe, but the degree to which we believe that God is God and that His Word is the key to everything in life determines our depth.

I have often told people to imagine being married to a truck driver who is only able to come home once a week for an hour. What kind of marriage would that be? It would be horrible. There would not be many benefits at all to that relationship. But that is how we treat God. The only time we really stop to think about Him, seek Him in our spirit, and attempt to connect with Him is at church. The bad part is that very few of us go to church every week, so the relationship may be even worse than the analogy I used. We have got to go deeper in our relationship with God if we want to enjoy the blessings of God to their fullest.

I don't want to be a little pool that you might see in the street after a rain. I don't want to be a kiddie pool that you have to blow up. I don't even want to be a pop-up pool. I want to be an Olympic-size pool. If possible, I want to be a lake. I want to experience all of the goodness of God, because I know that it will make me a greater blessing to all those around me.

Depth does not just happen, though. It requires sacrifice and commitment. You are not going to go any deeper in your relationship with God as long as you are still doing the same things you have always done to seek Him. We must make an effort to follow hard after Him, more and more each day. "For this very reason, make every effort to add to your faith goodness; and to goodness, knowledge; and to knowledge, self-control; and to self-control, perseverance; and to perseverance, godliness; and to godliness, brotherly kindness; and to brotherly kindness, love" (2 Peter 1:5–7 NIV).

I completely understand that Egypt is no fun. It is dry. It is dead. It is empty. It is your wife walking in and asking for a divorce. It is the doctor's diagnosis of a terminal illness. It is a pink slip at work. It is finding out that your worst fears have come true. It is so easy to want to just give up and die. The scorching heat of our situation would surely cook us quickly and end our misery, but we have to remember that He is the God who makes streams in the desert. If you look with your eyes and lean on your understanding of the desert, you will surely be consumed by it and overcome by it.

But Proverbs 3:5 teaches us to *not* lean on our own understanding. Instead, we are to lean on the promise that God is not overcome by our desert. In fact, He created the desert and allowed you—perhaps even led you—into the desert to force you to trust as you never have before. He is forcing you to live by faith by taking everything else away. He is pushing you into His love and His grace and His power by taking away anything and everything that you have put your trust in.

Here in the desert, you will be changed. Here He will force you to dig and dig deep. The simple mantras of years of Sunday school will not be enough. The Bible verses you learned to get a ribbon in vacation Bible school won't hold you now. The prayers of your wife or your grandmother cannot sustain you. These are all too spiritually shallow for you. They will not be enough. They will not get you through this desert. But if you, yourself, begin to dig deep to find the waters of greater truth, God will begin to bubble up water from under the dry ground. Dig a hole. Dig a pool. God is enlarging you so that you can hold more blessings.

Do you understand? Do you get it? The deserts you find yourself in during your time on this earth, are orchestrated by God. They are not meant to destroy you. On the contrary, they are intended to prepare you for greater blessings. Take your eyes off the sands of Egypt and look past them to the hills of Canaan, the land flowing with milk and honey. Dig deep in your relationship with God, and the desert will not be your destination. It will only be a stopover, for you are destined for more than you could ever imagine.

Thank God for your desert. Thrust your hand into the hot sand and embrace it as the instrument by which God is enlarging your capacity to be blessed. Know that He would not work to enlarge you if He was not going to fill you with every spiritual blessing.

"In all my prayers for all of you, I always pray with joy because of your partnership in the gospel from the first day until now, being confident of this, that he who began a good work in you will carry it on to completion until the day of Christ Jesus" (Philippians 1:4–6 NIV).

Chapter 4

Ups and Downs of the Journey

Change Is Not Enough

You are too small right now to hold what God has for you. God's plans for you exceed who you are as a person right now. He is blessing you, true. But what He really wants to do is more than you can handle right now. It might corrupt you. It might lead you to become so secure that you forget to pray. It might lead you to become so arrogant that you forget to praise. The blessings you are receiving right now do not compare with what God wants to do for you a year, two years, or ten years from now.

What hope we have as believers! Come what may, tomorrow is always good, because we are one day closer to the great things God has promised. Even when we arrive at the place of great blessing, God will simply enlarge His plans so that we have a hope of something even greater from God. If He gave it all to us right now, the blemishes of our hearts and characters would not be able to handle that kind of success or blessing. He is cleansing us, digging us out, creating a pool by which to flood us with His goodness. This journey is the plan of God for our lives.

You have to allow God into every area of your life so that He might cleanse you of anything that keeps you from His great plan. If you try to change one area of your life but refuse to let another area be cleaned out, that unclean area will affect the rest. Sometimes people fall into this idea that if they get things right in one area, God will somehow turn a blind eye to the other stuff. God will surely reward you for the change you have made. He will give you credit for the effort you have put forth. You are changing. At the same time, He is not going to ignore the other stuff that you think He can't see. You can't start going to church but continue an adulterous affair. You can't praise God about one thing in life and then, with the same lips, curse God in anger because He did not do what you wanted in another area of life. Improvement is change, but change is not enough. We must submit ourselves to God for more than change. We must allow Him to remake us into a new creation.

"And no one pours new wine into old wineskins. If he does, the wine will burst the skins, and both the wine and the wineskins will be ruined. No, he pours new wine into new wineskins" (Mark 2:22 NIV). When wine was poured into wineskins, it caused the wineskins to expand. If the wineskin had already expanded a great deal from use, new wine would cause it to expand even more, making it so thin that it would burst, and all of the wine would fall onto the ground.

This is why God says we must be made new. The old things in our lives have stretched our thinking in ways that our thoughts don't need to go, and the people of our past have stretched us in directions where we are not comfortable. All of this will cause us to be too thin, and the weight of new blessings will expand us to the point that we will burst. Our spirits will burst. Our hearts and lives will burst. Our old ways of thinking and handling situations will not allow us to hold the new ways of God. Our old patterns of thought will not allow us to hold His blessings. Our old way of choosing friends, boyfriends, and girlfriends will surely cause the wine of God's blessings to be poured out onto the ground. We must be made new.

If we want to keep the "wine" of God in our lives, we must not work to simply change a few things here and there; we must be radically transformed. We absolutely *must* think, respond, and act differently. We must surrender to the idea that we need a fundamental change in who and what we are. If we don't work to become completely different individuals by allowing God to invade every area of our lives, we will not enjoy, much less find, all the plans that God has for us.

"May God himself, the God of peace, sanctify you through and through. May your whole spirit, soul and body be kept blameless at the coming of our Lord Jesus Christ. The one who calls you is faithful and he will do it" (1 Thessalonians 5:23–24 NIV).

The plans of God are not for lightweights or sissies. He intends to make you great. He is at work, doing things in and through your life that are beyond your comprehension. A great person does not live and die only to be forgotten. A great person lives on in the memories of those they influenced. Those memories continue to bring peace, wisdom, and the warmth of love for generations.

A great person changes bloodlines so that his children and his children's children do not face the same battles he had to face. A great person is like a tree that takes the heat of the sun so that others might stand in its shade. A great person produces fruit, in season and out of season, for the weak and the weary. He gives strength, hope, power, love, and mercy to those the world has forgotten. He does the work of God on this earth and enjoys the feeling of knowing that his life has made a difference. A great person only becomes great with the help of God.

When we submit ourselves completely and fully to God so that He radically changes the DNA of our souls, he sets us free from the old junk so that we might become something new, something great.

This is a path that the halfhearted soul stumbles and falls on. Such a soul is not sturdy enough. We must be changed through and through, and this can only be accomplished by God. We are not holy. Our sinfulness is natural, and because it is natural, we don't see it. We sin as easily as we breathe. No one has to teach a two-year-old how to lie. It comes naturally. We don't have to teach a child selfishness. It comes naturally. We don't have to teach a young person how to scheme to get his way. It comes naturally. Sin is natural. Sin is so much of who we are that we don't even recognize it.

Everyone is sinful, so who has the purity of vision to point it out? No one but God Himself, who is truly holy and pure, is able to point out to us that which is sinful in us. We have known sin since our conception, and we see nothing wrong with it until God points it out. We only know that sin is sin when God tells us it's sin. Otherwise, we would be a huge society of lazy, selfish, hedonistic pigs, thinking there was nothing wrong with us. We need God to cleanse us, to dig us out completely, through and through. We need to be made new.

Some of us are not enjoying the plan God has for us, because we are still holding on to old ways, old mannerisms, old wisdom, old prejudices, old fears, and old treasures. We are still holding on to old dreams and expectations. We are still holding on to old boyfriends, drugs, and visions. Even when we are not hanging out with those people, taking those drugs, or settling for those old visions, our thoughts of them haunt and distract us. They get us off course and keep us from the path that God wants for us.

Resisting that which we know God does not want in our lives is good, but in order to embrace the all-encompassing plans of God, we must allow Him to cleanse us from the desire for those things. Resistance is good. But our goal must be to let God bring us to a newness that no longer has to fight to resist the former things.

It's not that we suddenly have the holiness of God and are unable to be tempted by sin. As we grow in the Lord, temptations from our former lives should pass away. There will be new battles and new temptations with every spiritual step, and we must keep walking away from our current temptations as we are continually made new. If I am growing, today's temptations should not continue to tempt me in the future. There are some addictive behaviors that may tempt us for a long time, but as we are made new, our ability to resist grows stronger. "See, I am doing a new thing! Now it springs up; do you not perceive it? I am making a way in the desert and streams in the wasteland" (Isaiah 43:19 NIV).

Our old habits can still flare up when we are under stress or when we feel afraid or insecure. Old visions of our former destinies can haunt us, and then we feel like failures. There has to be a moment in our lives when we decide to break free. Sometimes people think that if they start going to church or reading the Bible—or books like this one—their good intentions will break them free, but this is not true at all.

"That night Jacob got up and took his two wives, his two maidservants and his eleven sons and crossed the ford of the Jabbok. After he had sent them across the stream, he sent over all his possessions. So Jacob was left alone, and a man wrestled with him till daybreak. When the man saw that he could not overpower him, he touched the socket of Jacob's hip so that his hip was wrenched as he wrestled with the man. Then the man said, 'Let me go, for it is daybreak.' But Jacob replied, 'I will not let you go unless you bless me'" (Genesis 32:22–26 NIV).

Jacob had been a trickster. The meaning of his name, "the supplanter," reflects this. With the help of his mother, he deceived his father and received a blessing that belonged to his older brother. His brother, Esau, wanted to kill him for this, and Jacob had to flee. During his escape, Jacob lay down on a rock and began to dream. In the dream, God came to him, and Jacob pledged himself to God. Then he continued on his journey, and God blessed him greatly.

One day, God told Jacob to go back to his family. He was terrified, of course. The last time he'd seen his brother, his brother had wanted to kill him. When he sent his men ahead to spy out the land, they came back to say that his brother was coming with an army. Jacob was afraid and began to send gifts ahead to his brother. The Scripture says that he said to himself, "Perhaps I can pacify him with these."

Jacob had given himself to the Lord and was doing his best to follow God in his new commitment—a commitment that had brought many, many blessings. But when he got into a situation of stress and fear, he went right back to what he had always done: manipulation.

Because of this, God ordained a moment where He allowed Jacob to wrestle with an angel. The wrestling match was God's way of trying to get Jacob to leave the ways of his past and follow Him more fully. Jacob resisted, because that was how he had always handled such situations. The angel touched his hip, causing it to pop out of its socket. Jacob realized that if he didn't do things God's way to receive His blessing, life was going to be painful. He took hold of the angel and refused to let go. It was a surrender. God changed Jacob's name to Israel, and he became the Father of the twelve sons who would form the twelve tribes of Israel.

What a wrestling match! When God wrenched his hip, it was clear to Jacob that unless he made a change, he would never be free of his past.

Some of us have been wrestling with God for a long time. We have endured the pain of not doing things His way, but we continue to fight to do things our own way. We maintain justification for bad behavior. We claim that we can continue to act this way because our spouse or children act a certain way. We stress and worry and justify our behavior by saying to God, "You just don't understand the pressure I'm under." (That's funny, right?)

The truth is that there must be a break from our old values. We must break from our old ways of feeling insecure and learn to find security in Christ. We must forget our old ways of finding comfort in people and learn to be comforted by the Holy Spirit. We must stop propping up our self-image by catering to people who judge us the wrong way—just so they will like us. There has to be a break.

"For God did not give us a spirit of timidity, but a spirit of power, of love and of self-discipline" (2 Timothy 1:7 NIV). The Holy Spirit of God gives us the power to be self-disciplined. Reading the Bible more often is great. Going to church is awesome. Praying each day, more than just before a meal, is fantastic. But to break free from your past, you must set your mind and refuse to go back to that place.

Begin to discipline your mind to handle things the way He teaches us to handle them. Bless your enemies. Overlook offenses. Let nothing out of your mouth except what builds others up. Make a decision. You are the only one who can make up your mind. God has given you the power to do it, but only you can take hold of that power and break free.

Wrestling makes us tired. We try to hold on to people and ways and habits because they give us a false sense of security or love, but the truth is that we still don't feel secure or loved. Break! Break out now! Make a decision. Plant yourself like a rock on the promises of God. Draw upon the power of the Holy Spirit, and discipline yourself to think according to Scripture and according to God's promises instead of the Devil's lies. Take hold of God, and you will be changed just like Jacob. You will be changed and given a new spiritual name and a new destiny. You will enter the stage of life where your God-planned destiny begins, life becomes fulfilling, and your heart finds joy.

Make a decision. Make it right now. You have known for so long that these things of the past were holding you back. Break free! Write it down. "I will no longer be controlled by …" Put it on the fridge. Put it in your Bible. Tell your spouse that you are committed to change. Pray, pray, pray! Ask the Lord for power to discipline yourself, and then let the rain begin. Let the floods rain into your life. You will no longer be who you used to be, but you will become the person God designed you to be. You will be the person you have always wanted to be. The power is already in you. You can do it. Rain, God, rain!

Affections

> The child grew and was weaned, and on the day Isaac was weaned Abraham held a great feast. But Sarah saw that the son whom Hagar the Egyptian had borne to Abraham was mocking, and she said to Abraham, "Get rid of that slave woman and her son, for that slave woman's son will never share in the inheritance with my son Isaac." The matter distressed Abraham greatly because it concerned his son. But God said to him, "Do not be so distressed about the boy and your maidservant. Listen to whatever Sarah tells you, because it is through Isaac that your offspring will be reckoned. I will make the son of the maidservant into a nation also, because he is your offspring." Early the next morning Abraham took some food and a skin of water and gave them to Hagar. He set them on her shoulders and then sent her off with the boy. She went on her way and wandered in the desert of Beersheba. (Genesis 21:8–14 NIV)

God promised Abram a son as part of the promise of becoming a great nation. But his wife was barren and unable to have children. As many people did in those days, she gave her maidservant to her husband, and the maidservant, Hagar, gave birth to a boy for Abram.

Abram loved this boy. He was his son. He was his pride and joy. They walked and talked together and loved one another. However, God revealed to Abram that his son Ishmael was not the son by which God would make Abram into a great nation. In fact, God's promise was that He would give Abram a child by his wife, Sarai.

Fourteen years later, Sarai gave birth to Isaac. Now Abram had two sons. One son was born out of a lack of faith, and the other son was the promise of God. Abram loved both. So later, when Sarah wanted to get rid of Hagar and Ishmael, it was very troubling for Abraham. He loved Ishmael. They were bonded. But God told Abraham that he would take care of Ishmael, even though he would be gone. Abraham had to release his affection for Ishmael and give all of his affection to Isaac in order for God's promise to come to pass.

A person is defined by his affections. The things in this life that receive our affection will pull us and influence us in one direction or another. We will become the person our affections dictate. A man who gives all of his affection to his work will let that affection dictate his time and goals in life. A woman who gives all of her affection to shopping will spend all that she has. A minister who gives all of his affection to the church will lose his own children. We must be careful of the affections we allow ourselves to form.

Because our souls are full of sin and corruption, we tend to have unhealthy affections. Whether it is a sinful affection where we choose to do things we know we shouldn't, or an affection of iniquity where we choose poor techniques to deal with insecurity and loneliness, we do not choose affections well. It is a natural part of the human experience, because we are born into sin.

When God begins to call us to something new, He must change our affections. He has to draw us toward something new. We have to let go of the old affections. We must release them into the desert. We have to let go of the things we love in order to be able to receive blessings from the One who loves us. Every affection that competes with your affection for God becomes an enemy to God's most wonderful plan for you.

Jesus made a radical statement in the gospel of Luke: "Large crowds were traveling with Jesus, and turning to them he said: 'If anyone comes to me and does not hate his father and mother, his wife and children, his brothers and sisters—yes, even his own life—he cannot be my disciple'" (Luke 14:25–26 NIV).

To say that Christ wants us to hate our mothers and fathers goes against all of His other teachings and against the Ten Commandments, so we know that there is more to this statement. Jesus often said things like this to shock people into giving Him their attention, but He was just making a point. In those days, if a child followed a path that his parents did not approve of, it was said that he hated his parents. At that time, following Jesus was about to become very unpopular, and it still is today. Jesus was simply making the point that our love for Him cannot be surpassed or even matched by our love and affection for anyone or anything else in this life. Our greatest love by far must be for Him, while everything else must receive much less of our affection. And God will challenge this. He will challenge our affection for other things in our lives—even good, wholesome things.

He will put you in places where you have to choose. There will be times in your life where you will have to choose between following Christ and pursuing something else that has your affection. That "something else" may not be bad or sinful. It is just not God. You may have to release a boyfriend or girlfriend. You may have to release a job or security or friendships in order to follow God and what He has for you. Each time God challenges your affection for other things in your life, it's an opportunity for you to let go of anything that would hinder, slow down, or kill the plans God has for you.

Abraham made a difficult choice to let Ishmael go out into the desert so that God's plan through Isaac would not be damaged. God would continue to challenge Abraham. In fact, I believe one of the most difficult challenges we read about in the Bible was another time when God challenged Abraham's affections.

"Some time later God tested Abraham. He said to him, 'Abraham!' 'Here I am,' he replied. Then God said, 'Take your son, your only son, Isaac, whom you love, and go to the region of Moriah. Sacrifice him there as a burnt offering on one of the mountains I will tell you about'" (Genesis 22:1–2 NIV).

I have read, taught, and preached on this passage many times, but as a father of three boys, I still get a strong ache in my chest when I talk about it. Can you imagine God asking you to sacrifice your own child?

Oh, I know a lot of people will say, "Well, things were different in the Old Testament."

I don't care what it was like in the Old Testament. A father still loves his son. We know that Abraham loved Ishmael tremendously. But as much as he loved Ishmael, he knew that Isaac was the son of God's promise. He was the miracle baby that had come from him and Sarai when they were old. Sarai had been barren her entire life. Suddenly God promised a child, and Sarai had a little boy.

Before Isaac was born, Abraham had cried out to God in despair because he did not have an heir to whom he could leave his inheritance. God heard his cry and answered his prayer. Isaac was the promise. Isaac was Abraham's destiny. All of the promises God had given to Abraham were wrapped up in this little boy. If Abraham sacrificed him, he would be sacrificing not only his son but his life, his destiny, and his promise.

I would have argued. I would have screamed. I would have fought God. I would have exploded in anger, and then I might have tried to calm down and sweet-talk the Lord into changing His mind. To sacrifice my son—my only son, my miracle son, the son of the promise—would have been more than I could handle.

But Abraham handled it with obedience and trust in the Lord. "Early the next morning Abraham got up and saddled his donkey. He took with him two of his servants and his son Isaac. When he had cut enough wood for the burnt offering, he set out for the place God had told him about" (Genesis 22:3 NIV).

Early the next morning? *Early* the next morning? Are you kidding me? Abraham just obeyed. He took his son out to the place that God had shown him. He tied him up. He raised his knife high in the air, poised to come down hard on the chest of the baby boy he had held so close for so many years. He did not hesitate. Seriously?

Perhaps one of the most amazing things about this story is that Isaac was not a little boy. Of course, we know as parents that our babies will always be our babies, but they do grow up. We really don't know how old Isaac was when Abraham took him out and tied him up, but the original language implies a boy between his teen years and early adulthood.

Meanwhile, Abraham was a very old man. The only reason he was able to tie this boy down was because the boy let him. Isaac would have been plenty strong enough to keep his elderly father from tying him to the altar. But Isaac just submitted.

Abraham submitted to God when God asked him to sacrifice his only son. Isaac submitted to his father, Abraham, and let him tie him to the wood. We see in this scene the product of a father/son relationship that had produced obedience and submission without question. As much as Abraham trusted his heavenly Father, Isaac trusted his earthly father. What lessons must have been taught in that home! The character of the father has passed down to the son.

What lessons do we teach our children? We are trying to teach them that God has a plan for their lives and that they can do anything through Christ who gives them strength. This is a great lesson, but unless they learn to obey the Word of God, the complete fulfillment of God's plan for them will never be realized. We must teach our children to obey the Word of God, even when they don't understand or agree with God's direction. If they can learn to do this, then what can the Devil do to them? They will always be resting in the shadow of the Almighty. They will always be under His protection and under His blessing.

If God blessed someone who loved the gift more than the giver, then He would be enabling that person to have other gods in his life. The gift would become a destructive force that would bring him down. In your journey with God, you must expect times when God will challenge your affections. He will challenge you to sacrifice blessings that He Himself has given to you. These challenges will reveal to you where your affections lie.

Perhaps you serve the wants of your wife or your children before you serve the commands of God. Perhaps your affection lies more with religion than with God. Perhaps your career is more important than your faith. Perhaps your sports are just a little too important, and you act, well, not quite the way God would want you to when the refs make a bad call. (I think I just stepped on my own toes.)

There will be times on this journey when God will remove His blessing to see if you love Him—or if you just love what He can do for you. Too many of us use God as a sugar daddy, running to Him and expecting Him to hand over His wallet or the keys to the car whenever we want.

Meanwhile, we show no respect and no honor to the One who has given us everything. No, God is not your sugar daddy.

At times, He will challenge you and, seemingly, cut you off. These will be seasons of your life without blessing. We hate these seasons. We think God is being mean during these times. But He is not taking us through these times to be mean. He does it for us. He does it to allow us to see into our own hearts. God opens our hearts, and our true character is revealed during a time without blessing. Then we will realize that we really do love Him, that we really do praise Him in the good times and the bad. Or we will realize that we have been using Him and that we don't love Him as the most important person in our life. We will realize that we have loved Him like we love our nearest ATM machine.

> When they reached the place God had told him about, Abraham built an altar there and arranged the wood on it. He bound his son Isaac and laid him on the altar, on top of the wood. Then he reached out his hand and took the knife to slay his son. But the angel of the Lord called out to him from heaven, "Abraham! Abraham!" "Here I am," he replied. "Do not lay a hand on the boy," he said. "Do not do anything to him. Now I know that you fear God, because you have not withheld from me your son, your only son." (Genesis 22:9–12 NIV)

Abraham ultimately received the promises of God, because he proved that his affection belonged to God and not God's blessings.

Where do your affections lie? Is God your true love? We have to remember that this "thing" with God is not a business transaction. It is not a contract we are signing to buy a house or a car. It is a relationship. God desires a relationship like we have with those we love in this life. The only difference is that when we love Him, the love He returns is extravagant.

This is the journey. This is His plan. It is not about your profession, your marriage, your health, or anything else. These are all simply tools in the hands of the Potter to mold you into someone devoted to God. He will use your friends and your enemies. He will use your health and your sickness. He will use the church and the world. He will use your spouse and your children. He will use those who have loved you, and He will use those who have stomped all over you along the way. The destination is not a degree or a career, but a devotion to a God, whose love for you is unmatched. When you are ready to release everything else in life for Him, He gives you everything and more.

Seasons of sacrifice do come, and they are difficult, but the Lord is your goal, and He will sustain you. If He takes away some blessing, look deep into your heart to evaluate your affections. Discover if you love Him or if you love what He does for you. If your affection is set on anything other than Him, confess and repent, and then set your face to love Him more. Certainly, He is worthy of your love and affection more than anything else in this world. Trust Him today, and see if He does not return to your life more than you could ever imagine.

"Delight yourself in the Lord and he will give you the desires of your heart. Commit your way to the Lord; trust in him and he will do this: He will make your righteousness shine like the dawn, the justice of your cause like the noonday sun. Be still before the Lord and wait patiently for him" (Psalm 37:4–7 NIV).

A Call to Remember

"So Abram went up from Egypt to the Negev, with his wife and everything he had, and Lot went with him. Abram had become very wealthy in livestock and in silver and gold. From the Negev he went from place to place until he came to Bethel, to the place between Bethel and Ai where his tent had been earlier and where he had first built an altar. There Abram called on the name of the Lord" (Genesis 13:1–4 NIV).

We must never forget that God was leading Abram during this journey. Every turn to the left and to the right, every step, every skip, every direction—all were determined by the Lord, not Abram. We read that God led Abram from Egypt to the Negev and blessed him greatly. Then

God sent him back the way he had come, and Abram found himself back at Bethel. He had been there before and had built an altar. God brought him back to the same place, the same altar, and once again Abram worshipped God.

It was the same place and the same altar, but it was anything but the same worship. God had deliberately brought Abram back to where he had already been. When God brings you back to places you have already been, there is a reason. He is calling you to remember. He may have you remember a word you received from Him. He may want you to remember a time when He sustained you through difficult circumstances. He may want you to remember a miracle He wrought on your behalf. Remembering is important to the Lord.

> Brothers, think of what you were when you were called. Not many of you were wise by human standards; not many were influential; not many were of noble birth. But God chose the foolish things of the world to shame the wise; God chose the weak things of the world to shame the strong. He chose the lowly things of this world and the despised things—and the things that are not—to nullify the things that are, so that no one may boast before him. It is because of him that you are in Christ Jesus, who has become for us wisdom from God—that is, our righteousness, holiness and redemption. Therefore, as it is written: "Let him who boasts boast in the Lord." (1 Corinthians 1:26–31 NIV)

I love the old hymn that goes something like this, "Count your many blessings … Name them one by one." This is not just an old song that your grandmother used to sing in church when you were too little to understand. This is a solid biblical principle.

We tend to live by what we can see. What is in front of us is what consumes us. Just look at the news cycle. Something is the biggest thing that has ever happened—until a day later, when something else has happened. Then *it* becomes the biggest thing in the world. We are moved by what is in front of us.

God calls us to take time to look back and remember the steps of yesterday and yesteryear. When we are controlled by what is in front of us, we celebrate the blessings and good things in front of our eyes. Problems arise when what is in front of us is not good. Arguments with our spouse and the words, "I want a divorce," may bring us so low emotionally that often we can't get up. The doctor's report, a crumpled car, a dead child—these are the times when what is right in front of our faces is too much. If we are honest, there is often more of the bad and the ugly in front of our eyes than the good and blessed. If we allow what we see to control us and dominate our moods and outlook on life, we are going to be very miserable people without much faith for the future. This is the shadow of death.

"Even though I walk through the valley of the shadow of death, I will fear no evil, for you are with me; your rod and your staff, they comfort me" (Psalm 23:4). Typically, when we read this passage, we focus on the fact that God is with us, but for a minute, let me turn your attention to the shadow.

Shadows make things darker by standing between you and the light. It is just a shadow, but it makes things seem darker. It feels as if God is further away, but it is just a shadow. The attacks of the Enemy are just shadows. As long as we hold on to our faith, they never become more than shadows. It is only when we allow the shadows to affect our thoughts, our moods, and our actions, that the attacks begin to prosper against us.

As a believer, all the Devil can do to you is what God allows Him to do. He is on a leash. He can only go where he is allowed and do what God allows. I love the story of Job, not because Job suffered as he did, but because Satan had to ask permission to do anything. This means that even in the darkest shadows, God is still in control. His promise is that He will not allow Satan to do more to you than what you can handle without giving you an escape. His promise is that no matter what happens, He will turn it around. What Satan intends for evil, God will use for good.

To keep this in our minds when the shadows are so dark is difficult. There is no doubt about this. But that is why, when Jesus taught the disciples how to pray, He first said, "Our Father, hallowed by Your name." To be hallowed is to be praised, to be lifted up. Our ability to praise God comes from remembering all that He has done. When we begin to praise God for all that He has already done in our lives, our faith will latch on to these words and give us strength. We must learn to hone our ability to remember the victories—no matter how large or small—that God has already given us.

In the middle of our crises, God will whisper in our ears, "Remember. Remember when you faced something like this before and you made it. Remember when you were so afraid that you didn't want to open your eyes. Remember when the stress was so much that you thought your heart was going to burst. I was faithful. Remember what the doctors said, but I proved them wrong. Remember when the valley was so deep, and you never thought you would come out alive, but you are still standing. Remember when you wanted to give up, and all you could do was cry. I cried with you and sustained you through that season." When God brought Abram back to Bethel, He was whispering in his ear, "Remember."

The Lord had been good to Abram the first time he'd come to Bethel. God had called to him and made him great promises. The first time at Bethel, Abram was on cloud nine, thinking of what it meant to be God's chosen man. When he'd first heard these promises, He had worshipped. He sang. He danced. He played instruments. He sang so loud that the Egyptians heard a sound in the distance. (This is just my own embellishment.) He was excited about what God had promised him, and he was on his way to enjoying a great life.

It was like a fantastic church service where the Holy Spirit moves dramatically. The preaching was good. The music was good. They even played his favorite song. It was just a wonderful service before the Lord. It was easy to worship. It was easy to smile. It was easy to lift his hands in praise. He sang with all of his might. Afterward, Abram traveled with his wife, Sarai, to Egypt and—can you believe it?—after such a great church service, he acted unfaithfully. He sinned. He messed up.

Isn't it amazing how we can worship God so thoroughly and sincerely and then walk right out the door and commit sin as if we have never heard of God? Worship is an intimate time with God and the Holy Spirit. It is a sweet time. It is a wonderful time.

In marriage, there are many men who will enjoy a time of intimacy with their wives and then go to work and be intimate with someone else. Intimacy does not equate with faithfulness. Intimacy is a wonderful part of the marriage, but it does not create in us a better person who is more faithful and more committed to the marriage. It is designed to help us move in that direction, but there are no guarantees.

Too many people have equated intimacy with faithfulness. They have entered into the house of God, raised their hands, shouted hallelujah, wept, laughed, and sung praises to God. They have developed a confidence in this worship experience, as if it proves their maturity—to the point that they believe it's not worth worrying about the sins they commit.

Imagine how you would feel if you found out that your spouse had an adulterous affair, even while continuing to make love to you. You would feel betrayed and hurt. The intimacy would be deemed worthless and fake. You would feel used.

The full meaning of our worship is not determined by how many tears run down our face or how long our hands are raised as we worship the Lord. Our worship is given substance by our deeds. Our adoration of God is proved in the way we live between services. Our actions, our thoughts, and our words are what give meaning to intimate worship. Is it real? Are we truly devoted? Or has God just become another one of our lovers? Anyone can worship when everything is good, and we can worship all day long and never experience any change that is fundamental to who we are. We could live for worship and never grow spiritually.

So, after Abram's incredible worship service, God led him to Egypt, where Abram feared for his life and sinned against God. His wife was so beautiful that he was afraid that the Egyptian Pharaoh might kill him so he could take Sarai as his own wife. To keep Pharaoh from killing him, Abram claimed that she was his sister instead of his wife. If Abram appeared to be the brother of Sarai, Pharaoh would not feel threatened by Abram and would not want to kill him. So, after God had chosen Abram and made such great promises at Bethel, after Abram had worshipped God with all of his heart and mind, he went to Egypt, lost his faith, and sinned against God.

How can we so quickly move from dedication to the Lord to dedication to self! We vacillate so easily back and forth that if we are not careful, it will become like the familiar ride back and forth to work: we will not think anything about it. Have you ever arrived at work and realized that you are so accustomed to the drive that your mind was not in it and you can't even remember driving there?

God has called us to love Him and Him alone. He is a jealous God. He does not want to share us, because He knows that He, and He alone, can heal us, provide for us, and save our souls from damnation. When God sees other things in our lives that are keeping us at a distance from Him, He becomes angered and fights for us, for our future and our eternity. He knows that worship in response to His promises is not enough to make us new. Unless we are changed and made new, the plans that God has for us will never come to pass.

So God took Abram back to Bethel. It is a call from God for Abram to remember the last time he had been there at Bethel with God. Knowing Abram's sin, God wanted him to remember His promises. Too often our sins cause us to forget God's promises. I especially appreciate this promise: "If we confess our sins, he is faithful and just and will forgive us our sins and purify us from all unrighteousness" (1 John 1:9 NIV).

I can easily confess to you that many times I am so overwhelmed with sorrow over my own sin that I lose sight of God's grace. I forget that He is slow to anger. I forget that He is gracious and compassionate. I forget that He was not ignorant of any sin I have committed—or will ever commit—when He died for me. I just forget. At times like these, God will call us to remember His promises.

Abram stood before God with remorse and guilt. He had given himself to God, only to betray Him almost immediately. God called upon Abram to remember His promises. This call to remember was also a renewing of those promises. God was saying to Abram, "I know what you have done. I knew you were going to do it. But I am faithful even when you are not. My love is not limited by your sin. Only you can limit how much of my love you will receive. Do not let your past sins steal your future promises. I will still make you into a great nation. I will still make your name great. I will still bless all nations through you. Forgive yourself, because I have already forgiven you."

I like to go to a local McDonald's to write. It helps me to get away from the office, put on some headphones, listen to some David Crowder, and commune with the Holy Spirit. As I write this at McDonald's, I think about the incredible grace that God revealed to Abram, and I want to stand on the table and shout, "Praise God! Praise Him for His love!

Praise Him for His mercy! Praise Him for His goodness! Praise Him for His promises!"

Wherever you may be today, and no matter how badly you think you have messed everything up, God is calling you back to Bethel. He is whispering to your spirit, "Remember my promises. Accept my forgiveness, and open your eyes to where I am taking you. My plans for you are not dead in the least."

Let go. His promise was made before you were born, before you were physically or spiritually able to sin against Him, and your sins today will not blot out His love or His promises. Praise the name of our Lord God Jesus Christ!

A Return to Bethel

God brought Abram back to Bethel, the place where he had been once before. The name *Bethel* means "the house of God." I love how God always brings us back to His house. For Abram, Bethel was a place where a stone altar stood. For us, every time we are made aware of God's promises in our lives, we are in Bethel.

Some might say that whenever God brings us into His presence, we are in Bethel. But how can we say that we are ever *out* of the presence of God when He has said to us that He will never leave us nor forsake us? His house, His presence, is always with us. Jesus taught us through His conversation with the Samaritan woman that connection with God comes through spirit and truth. Though God is always with us, we are not always in the right mind or the right spirit to be connected to Him. Though He never leaves or forsakes us, that doesn't mean that we will not forsake Him and forget Him. We are often too distracted or too cold to have any connection with Him. He never leaves us, but we can certainly ignore Him. This was what happened to Abram in Egypt.

When faced with the possibility of his own death, Abram did not put his trust in God but in his own ability to manipulate and deceive. We often do things like this. It's almost as if God is just going to sit there and let us destroy our lives by our own vices, as if He doesn't care. God loves us too much to just sit back and watch us destroy our own lives. If God had let things alone and let Abram just ruin himself, everything would have been lost. But God, in the face of Abram's in-your-face disobedience, was gracious. Instead He sent a plague to Pharaoh.

"But the Lord inflicted serious diseases on Pharaoh and his household because of Abram's wife Sarai. So Pharaoh summoned Abram. 'What have you done to me?' he said. 'Why didn't you tell me she was your wife? Why did you say, "She is my sister," so that I took her to be my wife? Now then, here is your wife. Take her and go!' Then Pharaoh gave orders about Abram to his men, and they sent him on his way, with his wife and everything he had" (Genesis 12:17–20 NIV).

We don't know exactly how Pharaoh discovered that Abram was not telling the truth. Somehow God intervened. God saved the moment, and Pharaoh becomes the mouthpiece of God. Pharaoh chastised Abram. He was so angry at Abram and afraid of God that he kicked Abram out of the country. But before he kicked him out, he chewed him out for what he had done.

Can I stop right now and confess to you that there have been many times in my life when I have acted like Abram? In the face of God's goodness and blessings, I have put my trust in my own understanding. I have sinned. I have let fear and anger lead me down a path that should have destroyed any plans God had for me.

We all have done this. How many things have we done that should have caused God to pull back His wondrous plans for our lives? We have cheated, lied, and lost our tempers. We have used and manipulated people. Some of us have murdered, raped, and pillaged. Things like abortion and drunk driving have been our companion.

But God's love endures forever. It endures through our mistakes. It endures through our sin. It endures through our pure stupidity. It endures even as we sow our wild oats while running from Him. There is nothing you have done or could ever do that would cause God to erase His plans for you!

I love the story of the prodigal son. The Bible says that the son of a wealthy man took his share of inheritance and then went off to enjoy wild living. He worked very hard to destroy his own life and future. He ended up with a job feeding pigs. He was so hungry that he wanted to eat the pigs' slop. He thought to himself that there was no way he could go back to his father and maintain his rights as a son. He decided to beg his father to accept him as a servant instead. His actions had ruined any future enjoyment of his previous rights as a son, or so he thought. He got up to return to his father—not to be his son but to be a lowly servant.

I love what the Scripture says here.

> So he got up and went to his father. But while he was still a long way off, his father saw him and was filled with compassion for him; he ran to his son, threw his arms around him and kissed him. The son said to him, "Father, I have sinned against heaven and against you. I am no longer worthy to be called your son. But the father said to his servants, "Quick! Bring the best robe and put it on him. Put a ring on his finger and sandals on his feet. Bring the fattened calf and kill it. Let's have a feast and celebrate. For this son of mine was dead and is alive again; he was lost and is found." So they began to celebrate. (Luke 15:20–24 NIV)

The father saw his son while he was a long way off. I believe the father was looking out for him. This was only a parable and Jesus never said how long the son had been gone, but it doesn't really matter. Jesus was explaining the love of God. The father was still hoping, still believing that one day his son would come back. Maybe it had been three weeks, three hours, or three years. It does not matter. The father never gave up on his son.

And God, our heavenly Father, will never give up on you. Perhaps the path you have taken has landed you in Egypt or in the mud with the pigs. Come to your senses. You have not ruined your future, and God will use your past to teach you and build a foundation for your future. He is waiting and watching for you right now. The only reason you are reading this book right now is because He is calling you back to Bethel. He is calling you back to His dwelling, His presence.

May you never forget this compassion of God. Even as you try to live right and honor God, you are human, and this path that God is taking you on will find you in Egypt. Never forget that the Devil is a liar. He will try to convince you that your life is over and that God doesn't want you anymore. He will try to get you to give up and quit, to just jump off the deep end of sin and avarice. But remember that God never stops hoping for you.

This is so hard for people to believe. With everything we have done and all of the thoughts we have allowed into our minds, it's hard to think that God could take us back. Some of us might be like the prodigal son, thinking that God might take us back but only at a reduced position. This is not so.

Let's remove this idea from the personal arena and look at it from God's overall plan for humanity. We must never forget that God does not want anyone to perish and go to hell. God also knows that He is the only way for us to escape the consequences of our sin. So He must draw men to Himself. How does He do this? "For who among men knows the thoughts of a man except the man's spirit within him? In the same way no one knows the thoughts of God except the Spirit of God" (1 Corinthians 2:11 NIV).

If the Spirit of God is the only one who knows the thoughts of God, how can we know that God loves us before we have accepted Christ and received His Spirit? In theology, we call it *prevenient* or anticipatory grace. God puts a portion of His Spirit into us before we are saved in order to have a presence within us. Then we will be able to hear His voice when He calls. "No one can come to me unless the Father who sent me draws him, and I will raise him up at the last day" (John 6:44 NIV).

According to the apostle Paul, we have nothing good in us outside of the presence of God. If only the Spirit knows the thoughts of God, how can we hear God? We are unable to know the thoughts of God or to hear His words without the Holy Spirit. It is this portion of the Spirit that allows us to be drawn to Him. Without this, every thought and action would be made without Him.

Though each of us has this portion of His Spirit within us to be able to be drawn to Him, how does He draw us? How does this infinite God reveal Himself to finite beings? His methodology is found in the covenant He made with Abram.

He says that He will bless us. He will make our name great. He will bless other nations through us. God's plan for our life is not a set destination or profession or church. God's plan for our life is to draw us to Him that He might bless us. When people see our dedication to God and His dedication to us, their eyes are opened. He glorifies us with blessings.

We, then, use the blessings to glorify Him and let everyone know that our blessings have come from this loving, compassionate God. It gets people's attention. His plan is for our lives to be so blessed that it proves His existence to those who do not believe. Once they believe He exists, they will listen to the gospel of how God loves them and died for them while they were yet sinners (Romans 5:8). He draws them to His love and mercy.

Why, then, would God ever limit your future because of your past? Saving you from your mistakes and maintaining His awesome plan for your life fits into the overall plan He has for all of humanity. It is so easy to be like the prodigal son, thinking we have messed things up too badly to return. But when we consider God's plan for drawing all men to Him, it should only fortify the idea that God never stops hoping for us. He never stops believing. And when we finally come to our senses, He calls us back to Himself, back to Bethel. Praise God!

A Place of Revival

God brought Abram back to Bethel to remember.

There are times in life when everything has been brought so low that hope has died, and the possibility of something good coming along seems to be gone. At such times, we have only memories of good things. However, these memories have power to restore and renew. We are able to draw strength to move forward and find our faith again.

God called Abram to remember the love and grace that God had shown him when he first made a covenant with him. Abram had not handled Egypt very well. He had sinned against God, easily giving up on the promise of God. He might have felt as though everything was lost because of his poor judgment, but God called Abram back to the place where He had first expressed His love to Abram. This was the place of the covenant, and God was reminding Him of how much He had planned for him. But this time in Bethel, the situation was not the same.

I love to worship. I really wish that I could sing and carry a tune, but God has not blessed me with that kind of talent. I am very good, though, at making a joyful noise. I have the heart of a worship leader and the voice of a middle school boy going through puberty. Nevertheless, worship songs run through my mind. To stand before the Lord in worship—whether it's in church, the car, or my living room—brings life to my soul. When my life is going well and I am enjoying the blessings of God, worship is so sweet. But different seasons in our lives will bring us to different kinds of worship.

Do you remember that feeling you had when you came to church after committing the greatest sin of all? There was guilt and remorse. I have stood in church and wanted nothing but for God to end my life right then and there. I have been so amazed at the evil inside of me at times. When I stood before a holy God, covered in the blackness of my sin, I grieved as if I had died, as if my life was over.

Abram must have been feeling all of these things after Egypt. During his guilt and remorse, God invited him to a place of worship—*their* place of worship. God brought him back to Bethel, back to the house of God.

Too many people stay away from the house of God when they have sinned terribly. They stop going to church, and sometimes they never go back. But Scripture teaches us to never stop meeting together. In other words, make it a practice, a discipline, to go to the house of God. When we are suffering the effects of our own sin, we must learn that this is where God wants us.

Do you remember Peter and Judas? Judas took thirty pieces of silver to betray the Lord, and he is remembered as a traitor. He is despised for the horrendous act he committed. Peter, on the other hand, is held high in our opinion, but didn't Peter do the same thing as Judas? Judas did it for money. Peter did it for reputation. But they both betrayed Christ by rejecting and denying Him. Both betrayed their friend and teacher. The reason we see one as a traitor and one as a great leader of the early church is because of the difference in how they handled their sin.

After Judas betrayed Christ, he went to a tree, alone. This is exactly what the Enemy wants. He wants us to go to a solitary place, alone. Whether it is a physical place or an emotional place, he just wants us to be alone. He does not want us to have anyone to console us. He does not want anyone to encourage us. He does not want us in the presence of a forgiving God. He wants us to be alone in our guilt and remorse until it overtakes us. Judas hung himself. His body fell from the noose and broke open on the rocks. He died full of remorse, and he died alone.

Peter's story is different. Let's look at where we find Peter after his sin.

> Afterward Jesus appeared again to his disciples, by the Sea of Tiberias. It happened this way: Simon Peter, Thomas (called Didymus), Nathanael from Cana in Galilee, the sons of Zebedee, and two other disciples were together. "I'm going out to fish," Simon Peter told them, and they said, "We'll go with you." So they went out and got into the boat, but that night they caught nothing. Early in the morning, Jesus stood on the shore, but the disciples did not realize that it was Jesus. He called out to them, "Friends, haven't you any fish?" "No," they answered. He said, "Throw your net on the right side of the boat and you will find some." When they did, they were unable to haul the net in because of the large number of fish. Then the disciple whom Jesus loved said to Peter, "It is the Lord!" As soon as Simon Peter heard him say, "It is the Lord," he wrapped his outer garment around him (for he had taken it off) and jumped into the water. (John 21:1–7 NIV)

Where was Peter? He was with the disciples. After he had sinned, Peter went back to the church. I know they were fishing, but you know every church has to have a potluck every now and then. The point is that he returned to those with whom he had a relationship based on their common love and devotion to Christ. When he realized that Christ was there, he did not jump into the water to drown himself because of his guilt. He jumped in to get to Christ as fast as possible.

The presence of God is our place of restoration. It is our place of forgiveness. It is our place of renewal. This is what the house of God is supposed to be. It was there, at the church, where Peter received forgiveness and was able to put it behind him. Whatever sin you may have committed in your life, do not run from the church; run to it. It is at church that our spirit is quickened and we come to our senses. It is there that the blood of Jesus is applied to cleanse us of our guilty consciences. It is there that we weep, but we weep at the feet of a very merciful God. It is there that we are confronted with a love that forgives even our worst deeds. It is there that we pour out our hearts, and it is there that He heals our hearts. We must always return to the house of God.

God brought Abram back to Bethel. Abram stood there in front of the altar he had built previously as a celebration of the future promised by God. He remembered worshipping Him there with such exuberance and zeal. This time, though, there was not that same feeling. Now, he stood before God in his guilt. His head hung low, and he was depressed and sad. His soul was dark.

God said, "Do you know why I have brought you back here?" God did not take him to a new place but brought him back to the place where things had been so good before. This was God's way of saying, "I know what you have done. But I still love you. I still have a plan for you. I know your sin. I have rebuked you. I have corrected you. Now, I am bringing you back to me." The grace of God fell like a pouring rain that soaked Abram's heart and soul.

This is the kind of grace that words cannot express. It is a supernatural moment that words cannot define. This worship takes us deeper into the love and mercy of God, and it is defined only by praise, tears, and cries.

If you have ever experienced this kind of grace, you know what I am talking about. I have stood before God, knowing that my sins were more than enough for Him to leave me. David's words came to me, and I pleaded with the Lord, "Do not take your Holy Spirit from me" (Psalm 51). Sure, I could have sat there all day and quoted Scripture about how God will never leave me or how faithful He is to forgive, but part of me needed to acknowledge the fact that God remained with me by choice. He chose to stay with me. He chose not to take His Holy Spirit from me.

Never take the forgiveness of God for granted. He chooses to never leave us or forsake us. If you act like it is a hard and fast rule that you will be forgiven, you will approach God with a ungrateful spirit, as if He owes you something. The simple truth is that God could choose to remove all His blessings as a result of your sin; and He would be justified in doing so. Cry out to Him. Never take Him for granted. He *could* choose to stop holding you. He *could* choose to change the plans He has for you. But instead, as with Abram, He chastises in the realm of grace, rebuking and restoring in the same moment. Grace like this can only be appreciated through tears mixed with guilt, remorse, repentance, thankfulness, and amazement.

After we sin, God does not push us away, He draw us back to His presence and His church. This time, the worship is not the same, for we are changed. With tears of repentance, we cry out to God. We say the same things we did the last time we were in Bethel. We sing the same songs, but this time, the meaning is deeper. We are far more connected. We do not merely participate in the worship. Rather, we embrace with all of our heart the lover of our souls. Experiencing grace like this stirs in us a desire to honor God more than ever before. It makes us want to hold on to Him more, to seek Him more, to listen to Him more. And we are revived!

"We love because he first loved us" (1 John 4:19 NIV).

It is the love of God that draws us. It is the love of God that moves us. It is the love of God that convicts us. It is the love of God that covers us with grace. It is the love of God that keeps us, restores us, and strengthens us. There is nothing more powerful than love. It is His love, in relation to our sin, that amazes us. We are humbled, inspired, and motivated. We are revived.

Experiencing a deeper level of God's love awakens our broken hearts to life again. These deeper encounters of love will only be found when we deserve it the least. It's when we are the most unlovable that the depth of His love is made known to us. I do not say this as justification to sin because the result is a deeper love between us and God. I say this as a reminder that God's intention has always been to reveal His love to you.

Just because you sinned in "Egypt," as Abram did, don't think for a moment that God is tossing you out. He will use this moment in a magnificent way to reveal to you further just how far His love goes. If you have isolated yourself physically or emotionally, open your heart. God does not hate you. He desires to use your mistakes and sin to draw you even closer to His love. Leave Judas' tree. Let the noose hang empty. Return to God. His plans for you remain. If you return to Bethel, He will revive you again.

"Come, let us return to the Lord. He has torn us to pieces but he will heal us; he has injured us but he will bind up our wounds. After two days he will revive us; on the third day he will restore us, that we may live in his presence. Let us acknowledge the Lord; let us press on to acknowledge him. As surely as the sun rises, he will appear; he will come to us like the winter rains, like the spring rains that water the earth" (Hosea 6:1–3 NIV).

The plans of God for your life are not about His blessings. They are about God moving us into a spiritual place where His plans can be realized. This is difficult, because our sinful nature gravitates to the desires of the heart, which is a path that ends in the Devil's prison. We must seek the Lord and allow Him to prepare and position us for the desires of our hearts.

The difficulty is that this preparation includes times in our lives where God tears us to pieces. He lets us suffer. Sometimes this suffering is the result of sin. Sometimes we suffer even though we have not sinned. All suffering is for the purpose of maturing our hearts. If we will learn how to hold on to Him during the suffering, our knowledge and experience of His love and power will increase.

With each cycle of being torn apart and then healed, our love and dedication for Him will increase. Our desire for sin will dissipate. Our hearts will be stronger, our spirits fuller, our lives more ablaze for Him. When we return to the presence of God to repent and seek forgiveness, He never fails to lavish us with forgiveness and love—and revival. Revival begins at repentance with our knowing that His love has not diminished in the face of our sin, and this gives us a greater knowledge and appreciation of Him. We fall in love with the Lord again and again each time we are healed from sin.

In Scripture, God refers to Himself as the groom and the church as the bride. In this analogy, given to help us understand our relationship with Him, He does not refer to Himself as the husband and us as the wife. Instead He uses newlywed terms. When people are first married, the air is full of romance. They can't wait to see one another. They love being together. It is exciting and fresh. This is how God feels about us, always. His love for us is pure. It never becomes stagnant, as love can become in a marriage. We have a need, a desire for a love that is ever new. God is able to do this because of His character. We, on the other hand, slip into the marriage rut. We stop showing affection. We take each other for granted. We become more like roommates than lovers.

God does not want this kind of relationship. That is what revival is all about. It is God showing up with flowers and candy, expressing His love to us in a new way. Our sinful humanity is stubborn, and many times God must wound and then heal us in order to open our eyes to His always-increasing love for us. We must embrace this cycle of tearing and healing, injuring and binding. When we do, revival will become a regular part of our lives. Life with Christ will never become stale. Instead, it will always get better.

Let me add just a little word for those who are in the tearing season. The Scripture from Hosea above promises that God will come with healing in His hands as surely as the sun rises. No one wakes up in the morning wondering if the sun will rise. You can have that much faith that He will come to you. Even now, in your pain, celebrate, because healing is surely on its way!

The Purpose of Egypt

It's a long way to travel for a lesson, but our journey with God will carry us into many classrooms. In one classroom, the Lord will teach a particular lesson. In another, He will teach the follow-up. One relationship will bring one lesson, while another relationship allows the Lord to teach a different lesson. Jobs, churches, neighbors, friends, and enemies are simply classrooms where God stands at the chalkboards of our hearts and teaches us the lessons of life that we need to learn in order to enjoy all He has for our lives.

We must never forget that God is preparing our hearts for His plans. Without mature hearts, the blessings will become curses. We cannot just accept the changes of life as coincidence. These are deliberate turns to the right and to the left. The Lord is leading us through one classroom after another for the deliberate purpose of maturing our hearts. This is what Egypt was all about for Abram.

I often hear people say, "I don't know if God wants me to go here or there. I don't know if God wants me to do this or that." There are many times in life when we have choices. I don't believe God is always wanting us to choose one over the other. As we saw with Abram, sin does not stop God from working to accomplish His plan in us, and neither will one choice over another.

Obviously, sin is never something that God wants for us. If you are sinning and you have somehow convinced yourself that this is God's plan for you, you need to stop and take inventory of your heart. Return to God fully. When choice A and choice B are both good options, it is possible that the Lord is prepared to teach you the lessons needed at either place. He can mature you and bless you, whether you choose door number 1 or door number 2.

When Joshua took over for Moses, God told him that his only goal should be to please Him (God), and that if Joshua would do this, God would then bless him wherever he went. He would bless him to the right or to the left, this way or that, through door number 1 or door number 2. "Be strong and very courageous. Be careful to obey all the law my servant Moses gave you; do not turn from it to the right or to the left, that you may be successful wherever you go" (Joshua 1:7 NIV). God's emphasis for Joshua is not on what he does or where he goes but on whom he seeks.

As long as we earnestly seek God and His way, acknowledging Him with our praise and worship, His plan for our life will manifest. Wherever you go, know that there will be some places that are more difficult than others. God has led you there for the purpose of teaching you something. The good news here is that no matter where you are, God's plan is for your success. Moses found success in the desert. Joseph found success in a prison. Daniel found success surrounded by hungry lions. Paul and Silas found success in the torture chamber. The thief found success on the cross. We can never allow our circumstances to convince us that God's plan for our lives has been suspended. Every place you go, good or bad, God will use to bring out your destiny.

Abram was not sent into Egypt so that God could see what was in his heart. God already knows our hearts and minds completely. He is never fooled, surprised, or deceived. But we, on the other hand, are easily deceived. Abram was sent into Egypt, not so that God could determine his heart, but so that Abram could see what was in his own heart.

We are easily taken in by lies, even if the lies have come from our own mouths. Have you ever known anyone who has lied so much about something that he begins to believe his own lie? The "Egypts" of our lives are not for God's benefit but for ours. We must have times in our lives where we are able to see who we truly are. Egypt is the place where our level of faith and trust is revealed. We are unable to see the level of our love until that love is challenged. We can't see the depth of our trust in God until that trust is challenged.

Let me give you an example. It's easy to love your baby. Babies are cute and cuddly. But how well do you love them when they are teenagers who rebel against everything you say? We need places like Egypt, or we will fool ourselves. Many people are convinced that they love someone enough to get married. It is much easier to love someone you see once or twice a week than someone who is always with you. It's easy to love someone when you don't have to talk about issues like money, children, and in-laws. We convince ourselves that we love someone, but the strength and depth of that love is revealed when they hurt us.

This is Egypt. Without Egypt, we fool ourselves into believing that we love God with all of our heart, soul, mind, and body. Our emotions are good liars. It feels like we love God with all of our heart, but we don't really know until we arrive at the difficult and stressful moments of life. I think if we could have interviewed Abram before Egypt, he would have affirmed his complete love and devotion to God. He was unable to see the frailty of his love for God until that love was challenged in Egypt. Rather than choosing to do things God's way, he betrayed God by choosing to deceive and lie. Only afterward was he able to see the true dimensions of his love for God.

"The heart is deceitful above all things and beyond cure. Who can understand it?" (Jeremiah 17:9 NIV). I remember the first time this Scripture really sank into my spirit. It taught me that I am able to lie to myself and fool myself better than the Devil himself, who is the Father of Lies. When I consider the evil deceitfulness found in the heart of Satan, and then realize that I can be just as deceitful with myself, I am amazed at the evil within me. Though I am a Christian, I am not perfect, and I do fail. I have failed many times.

One of our biggest failures as humans is to allow what we desire to cloud the Word of God. We will make up all kinds of reasons to do something that we know is wrong. Somewhere in the recesses of our spirit, the Sunday school lessons we learned remind us that what we desire is wrong, but we have an uncanny ability to ignore those thoughts. We not only proceed with the sin, but we justify it all the way. Our sinful desires and passions will push us away from the plans that God has for us.

I would define this as pure evil, and it is who I am. It is who we all are, without the influence of God. If I am able to deceive myself so much that I actually accept some precept that, in a different context, I would declare sinful, then how much evil is in my heart? The Holy Spirit in me desires that I obey and please God, yet the evil within me can sometimes take control and pursue things that I know are grotesque in the eyes of God. Yet, I do it anyway.

This evil is no small part of our lives. It is huge. The good news is that the Holy Spirit in us is always stronger. There is no temptation that we can't resist by the power of the Holy Spirit, but maturity is the key to following the Spirit. Maturity allows me to hear and submit to the Holy Spirit, ignoring the sinful nature and all its evil desires.

In our arrogance, we think we are basically good people. However, at times we shock ourselves by the sins we commit, even as we convince ourselves that it's okay. I think it is important for us to understand the evil within. I am not saying that we are all demon-possessed and somehow transform into Halloween's Jason or Elm Street's Freddy Krueger. I am saying that evil is easy for us.

We tend to think of evil as murder or rape or adultery—and certainly those things are evil. But isn't a lie evil? Isn't saying hurtful things in our anger evil? Evil is the absence of good, and only God is good. Therefore, anything we do that God is displeased with is evil.

Yet we can do these things and never consider for a minute that God is hurt by what we have done. We ignore God. We justify our sin by what others have done. We diminish our sin by thinking that everyone does it. Jesus was very careful to point out to us that lust will be judged the same as adultery. A lustful glance at a woman is evil. Letting our eyes move over the parts of a body other than our spouse's is offensive to God. Impure thoughts that run through our mind about someone are evil.

These are not just innocent thoughts. Though many other people might be thinking the very same thing, these thoughts are evil. These "harmless" glances will be judged the same as adultery.

Look at it backward. If we knowingly took someone's naked body into our arms—someone who was not our spouse—and touched them, kissed them, and had relations with them, would that be evil? Of course. Imagine how evil it would feel if it was your spouse cheating on you. No doubt, we would call *that* evil. Yet to God, the lustful glance and the act of adultery merit the same punishment. Jesus also said that anger expressed in a sinful way is no less evil than murder. Evil is easy for us.

We must adapt our definition of evil to parallel God's definition. Society has taught us to diminish the evil within because "everyone does it," "it's not that bad," or "it's not that big of a deal." We justify our sin by blaming others for what they have done, and we convince ourselves that our sinful reaction to their sin is somehow okay.

This is just not so. Christ is our example. He is our goal. The One who forgave those who rejected Him while He hung on the cross is the model we should use to guide our actions. If we don't face the evil within, we will not guard ourselves from it, and we will fall prey to this evil.

Do you remember the man whom God referred to as "a man after my own heart"? It was David, who was chosen by God to be the king of Israel, even though he was not a blood relative of the current king. David had the faith to face a giant without armor or spear. David, by the power of God, defeated that giant and cut off his head. David was so honored by God that he became a military power. David loved God so dearly that he wrote song after song to Him, and we now call his songs the Psalms. Yes, this David is the one that God said was a man after His own heart.

But evil rose up in this righteous man. He took another man's wife and she became pregnant. In order to disguise his sin, he murdered the woman's husband. Then, with incredible audacity, he took the woman in as his own wife, acting as if he was doing a good deed because she was a widow. The sinful nature within him was able to put up a veil that did not allow him to see the evil he had done—until the prophet Nathan made him aware of it.

Too many of us have sin that is hidden. I don't mean hidden from God, because God always knows. I mean that we have hidden it from ourselves. We act as if everything is just fine, as if God has no issue with what we are doing or have done. It's times like these that we need Egypt to reveal what is in our own hearts.

God led Abram to Egypt in order to open his eyes as to what was in his own heart. Abram learned how quickly he might give up the promises of God. God had promised that through Abram's offspring he would become a great nation. But as soon as Abram desired his own life more than God's promise, he gave up that promise. He gave up the promise by giving up his wife in order to protect his own hide.

The purpose of Egypt was for Abram to see where he was weak and unfaithful. He was later chastised by Pharaoh. This was God's way of driving home the point. Abram had lied, sinned, and disobeyed God to protect what he wanted, forfeiting God's promise. To protect his own life, he gave up his wife and any children they might have had together.

Now, this is the place where so many people today would say, "Well, what did you want him to do? He would have been killed. Abram was right in what he did. Pharaoh took his wife. If Abram had died, how could he have had children? What about that preacher-boy?"

Well, I would point out to these brothers and sisters that God intervened and protected His promise to Abram by making Pharaoh aware that Sarai was Abram's wife. God did this even after Abram had sinned. If God protected the promise even after Abram sinned, wouldn't He certainly have protected the promise all the more if Abram had been faithful? In this situation, Abram acted as if God did not even exist—or at least as if God had no power to intervene on his behalf.

Let's keep in mind that Abram was very close to God. He was being led by God. He spoke to God. But when his fear became more prominent than what God had promised, he gave up the promise. If Abraham, who spoke with God, could hide from himself this kind of selfishness and lack of faith, what might we be able to hide from our own hearts?

Perhaps, we are hiding our insecurities, our lust, our jealousy, our unforgiveness, our drunkenness. We may have justified these things, pretending that God understands our sin and that He is somehow okay with them. We may have blamed others. Fortunately, in order to help us see these immaturities in our hearts, God will send us to Egypt. He will allow us to face a very difficult choice between what we want and what He has promised.

He will make us choose between an occupation we love and His promises of something better. We will have to choose between the person we "love," though the relationship makes the path to sin easy, and God's promise of someone who helps us move closer to Him. We will have to decide if we want to keep the anger that has allowed us to protect ourselves from hurt (or so we think) or if we want to let these things go in order to take hold of the promises of God.

What will you choose when you are asked to give up something you love, cherish, or feel like you absolutely need? All of these things may cause you to forfeit something better. Sometimes, we have to let go of what we have, accepting as truth something we can't see. Abram needed to let go of the life God had given him, subject himself to death at the hands of Pharaoh, and hold on to God's promise of a child with Sarai.

There may be some sin in your life that is giving you false hope. You may feel as if you can't live without this sin, but it is not pleasing to God. Nevertheless, God has something much better than anything you could imagine. Trust in Him! The alternative is what you have dreamed of and hoped for. Don't settle for anything less than what God has for you. All good and perfect gifts come from above. Never forget: God *is* faithful!

Relentless

Abram tried very hard to give up the promise God had for him. He lost faith. He lied. He showed contempt toward God by not trusting Him. So, why would God choose a man who was going to be so difficult?

We might think God should have chosen someone better, but God did not choose Abram because he was righteous. He chose Abram in order to produce a nation in which He could show His favor—for all other nations to see. God's hope was that when other nations saw the blessing upon His people, and when the nations heard His people acknowledging Him for these blessings, all would turn to Him.

God's plan was so much larger than this one man, Abram. God was setting forth a plan that would continue even to our day. This was the beginning of God's plan to save every soul, to cause everyone, from beginning to the end of time, to turn to Him. When Abram disobeyed, lied, and lost trust in God, certainly God could have moved on to the next person. We know that God destroyed all the earth, save Noah and his family, once before. But God had made a covenant with Abram. For the benefit of the entire human race, He was not about to let go of Abram.

Even as I write this, it strikes me as an awesome thought. Abram has messed up, yet God did not abandon Him. Abram was not God's overall objective, yet he was. God places the same importance on one person as He does on all people. Certainly we have a choice to let God's plans work through us, or we can totally reject Him. But let us consider God's relentless pursuit of us, even when we have messed up. Praise the merciful, wonderful God of Israel!

We have to see God's plan for our lives in this light. God wants to bless us so that through us He might do greater things and bring blessings to more people. The plans of God for your life are not isolated. They include other people. God never gives up on His plans for you, but His plans for you are part of a greater plan for everyone you will ever have any influence over.

Sure, He could accomplish the same thing through someone else, but that is not what He wants. You are a covenant partner. He made a promise. You are His child. You are His son or daughter, and the last thing He wants to do is discard you and move on to someone else who is easier to work with. What amazing grace! You may often feel discarded, but God's desire is to bless *others* by blessing *you* first. He could have done what He wants through anyone else, but He has chosen you.

You life has been orchestrated so that you are present in this very moment in time in order to reach specific people in your life, to help specific people that you will come in contact with. He has chosen you and no one else to be the husband to your wife or the mother of your children. His goal when He chose you was not just to bless other people but to also bless you.

God's plan for your life carries greater significance than you might think. His plan for you is bigger than you. God never blesses anyone just for that one individual. All of God's blessings have the end goal of blessing others. These big plans of God will never exclude you, no matter what you have done. You can reject Him, and you can reject His plans for your life, but He will never abandon you. He is relentless!

To accomplish both parts of His plan—blessing you and others through you—He must move your heart to a place where you will never forfeit His blessings and His plans, no matter the temptations, the fear, or the worry. When you forfeit what God wants to do through you and for you, you are forfeiting blessings that are intended not just for you but for others around you.

God could bless your children through someone else if He wanted to, but not without their suffering. You could give up, decide that it is too hard, and tell God to find someone else to work through. And He can and will, if you continue to refuse. But the cost of your refusal to obey His plans will cause suffering, not only in your life but in the lives of others as well. You may feel like you are the worst person, the worst mom or dad, or the worst friend, and you would love to crawl into a hole somewhere and forget everything—and God could still bless your friend. He could still bless your children, no doubt. He could still bring them to His plans for their lives, but not without their suffering.

If I gave up on being a dad because I felt like such a failure, God could bless my children and bring them to His plan for their lives, but they would suffer, because their dad would not be there for them as he should be. It would be more difficult for them to get to the place God has prepared for them. They would need more time to heal from the wounds I caused.

On the other hand, if I live as a blessing to them, allowing God to sculpt me, and living in His plans for my life, they will not suffer as many wounds. They will suffer less because of my obedience to His plans. They will be better prepared spiritually to receive God's plan in their own lives.

In case you might be missing the point, let me be blunt. *Your life is not about you! You are living for your loved ones' futures!*

If God has called you to be a teacher, He wants to bless you in such a way that you become a blessing to your students. If you do not allow Him to mold you so that you can hold these blessings, the children God intended to blessed through you will suffer. God can still bless them, but the suffering will make it difficult for them to experience God's plan for their lives. They will be behind. They will struggle. They will have to fight for blessings that would have come much easier if you had allowed God to do in you what He wanted to do. If God has called you to be a parent, there are blessings intended for your children that God intends to come through you. If you disappear physically, emotionally, or spiritually, God can still bless them, but they will suffer.

Everywhere you look in our society, we see people trying to overcome the pain they've incurred because the people around them—people God had destined to be a blessing to them—gave up on His plan. People work through insecurities because their dad left at an early age. They struggle with anger, trying to protect themselves from more pain, because of what mom did. They fight to do well in business, but to a fault, so they become workaholics, trying to prove to someone that they have worth—because all they heard growing up was how worthless they were and that they were never going to amount to anything.

You could give up right now and tell God it is too hard being sculpted and crafted into His vessel, but there are people around you who would suddenly have to fight through the pain caused by your forfeiture of God's plan. God has chosen you to be in their lives. He has chosen you to help them develop and heal. He has chosen you to protect them and give them wisdom. If you leave God, He will not abandon them, but their battles increase with every step you take away from God's plan.

"That's cruel. It's not fair. That's too much responsibility." These are things we might say as this is settling into our spirits. We wonder why God couldn't just let us live in isolation. Why did He have to connect us to people? Why did He give us children? Why did He trap us like this?

Have you ever felt trapped? Have you ever felt as though God has stuck you in a place that you cannot escape, though you desperately want to? If we are not careful, we can become bitter with God about this. But what God has trapped you into is the pathway to joy and peace and love. Maybe you want to quit because the journey you are on is just too hard. Even now, as you are reading these words, God has positioned you in a place where you just can't run away. There are too many things and too many people that your absence would affect. So you are stuck, trapped.

What we forget is that we don't know what would happen if we were not connected to people. What if you left the ministry? What if you left your wife? What if you left your job, your church, your life? You don't know what you would find outside of these connections. But God knows exactly what you would find. He knows where that separation would lead you, and He loves you too much to let you go. What you see as a trap is really a wonderful rod and staff keeping you from torturous times apart from God.

In the Twenty-third Psalm, David wrote about having no fear, even in the valley of the shadow of death. Why did he have no fear? He had no fear because He was comforted by the rod and staff of the Shepherd. The rod and the staff are not always warm and fuzzy, but they are blessed. These were tools that kept the sheep from just going wherever they wanted to go. They could not easily wander off. If they started going down the wrong path, the shepherd would reach out his staff and bring them back. If they were stubborn, he might strike them with the rod, causing enough pain to get them to move the right direction.

God has placed you within a circle of people and has given you affection for them. You love them, even if you don't always want to admit it. You are afraid that you are destroying them. You are afraid that you have failed them. You are wondering if their lives would have been better had you never come in contact with them, and you just want to run.

But the countenance of your little boy or girl reminds you that God has placed you in a family. Their paths to God's providence is greatly affected by you. They are family—whether they are your biological family, a church family, or a work family. They need God, and He has chosen you to be the example of Him. Don't run. They need you, and you need them. Let God's plan for your life happen. You will be incredibly blessed, and you will *be* a blessing.

There are going to be times in your life when your love for these people—be it for your husband, your baby, or your sister—will be the only reason you can find not to give up. That's okay. Let that be enough to stick it out. The shepherds of old often led the sheep through barren lands, but they never stopped searching until they found the green pastures. Let God's rod and staff comfort you, not because they are pleasant, but because they will keep you on the right path.

Because the plans of God for you carry such weight, He must mature you to the point where you never do what Abram did and forfeit His plan for your life just because you get a little stressed or discouraged. He is teaching you that the greatest plans for your life come only through Him. To receive these blessings, you must hold on to Him with all of your might. The journey you are on is intended to be the instrument by which God increases your ability to hold on to Him, no matter what.

He is revealing to you a plan that is so wonderful that you will be willing to suffer and sacrifice. He is bringing you to a place of relentless pursuit. Egypt is not proof that God doesn't care; Egypt is proof that God has a great plan for your life. He needs to send you to Egypt at times to allow you to see where you are not holding on to Him.

If you are currently traveling through Egypt today, find where your grip on God is weak, and strengthen it. He will not give up on you. He is relentless!

Holding On

Abram failed. He tried to hold on tighter to his own life than to God's plan. The stress, worry, and fear caused Abram to wander off. Pharaoh chastised Abram for what he had done. It was as if God Himself was chastising Abram. Abram knew that he had lied. He knew that he had not trusted the Lord as he should have. He knew that he had failed.

Failure is so difficult. I have stood in the presence of God after my own failures. Though I was standing in His presence, I was consumed with hatred toward myself. I wanted to punish myself severely for the things I had done. I have wanted to inflict serious physical pain on myself—or even take my own life. I have stood in my office or in an empty sanctuary, condemning and telling myself how horrible and worthless I am. I have wanted to completely destroy the person I was. Disgust, shame, sorrow—all of these emotions have flooded through me.

Then, in the middle of my personal flogging, I would remember that God was there with me. He would remind me of His promises, though I struggled to apply them because of my self-condemnation. Ultimately, these are the Scriptures that He puts in my heart: "Therefore, there is now no condemnation for those who are in Christ Jesus" (Romans 8:1 NIV). "If we confess our sins, he is faithful and just and will forgive us our sins and purify us from all unrighteousness" (1 John 1:9 NIV).

As I stand in the presence of God, thrusting daggers into my own soul, He says, "There is no condemnation for you here." All I want to do is condemn myself. I want to lash out against my own flesh. I want to run away. I want to die and forfeit everything, because I am so aware of my unworthiness. I say, "No, Lord. You can't bless me. I am evil before you. I am a horrible human being. You saw what I did. You heard my thoughts and my attitude. You saw the sin in my soul."

He replies, "My son, I love you. I forgive you. I still have great plans for you. Turn from your sin. Stop killing your own spirit. I have not spared you just to let you condemn yourself. There is no condemnation, only love and forgiveness."

The eyes of my spirit are turned from my own wickedness to gaze upon such brilliant grace. I am overwhelmed more by His great love, mercy, and grace than my own wickedness. In the courtroom of heaven, I stand before the Judge, and He offers me grace. Being fully aware of my sin, while at the same time being fully aware of His grace and tender mercies, melts my self-hatred. The rage held in my tight-fisted hands is released. My soul and my hands turn upward in praise. How great is this God who loves me even now!

Whatever you have done, no matter the failures you carry, no matter the sin that still haunts you with guilt, turn your life completely over to Him. In Jesus Christ, and in Him alone, there is found an incredible grace in the midst of your sorrow. Your anger will be released in tears, and your tears will turn to joy. This moment of confession in the courtroom of heaven will cause you to fall in love with Christ even more than ever before. The soul within you that you wanted to destroy will be revived. What started in sin will end in praise!

This is how Abram felt when he found himself in the place he had been before, but this time it was different. He stood there, stained with guilt yet covered in forgiveness. This time he realized that God's love for

Him was more than he had thought possible. Through this moment of revival, Abram drew near to God and became more faithful, more dedicated. He set his mind to never let go of God. Though he would fail again, each revival moment, like that one, would strengthen his faith and his walk.

"So Abram went up from Egypt to the Negev, with his wife and everything he had, and Lot went with him. Abram had become very wealthy in livestock and in silver and gold. From the Negev he went from place to place until he came to Bethel, to the place between Bethel and Ai where his tent had been earlier and where he had first built an altar. There Abram called on the name of the Lord" (Genesis 13:1–4 NIV).

Abram called upon the name of the Lord in the same place he had been before he went to Egypt. But this time when he called upon the name of the Lord, he was more aware of God's love, more aware of His grace. He knew more of God's love.

These moments happen time and again. They cause us to become relentless in our pursuit of God above everything else. This was God's purpose for Abram's journey into Egypt. God allowed Abram to see his own sin, to see how quickly he was ready to let go of God's plan in exchange for his own life. At the same time, Abram also saw the providence and protection of a God who loved him.

The next time you are in Egypt, do not let the Devil fool you, saying that God's plan for you is dead. No, this is just part of the journey. When you fail, let your anger subside long enough to look up to the throne of heaven, where the love and forgiveness of God will overshadow anything you have done. Let that love sink in. Bathe in it. Soak in it. Receive it. Let it draw you closer to Him. Be revived. Live again. Hold on to God no matter what, and He will deliver you. Failure is never the end of God's plan for your life. Failure is part of the journey. When we carry our failures to God, they will always lead to a stronger commitment and dedication to God. They prepare us to hold on to God's promises above everything else in life.

The Point of Death

The word *revival* means "to be revived, to be brought back to life." As a pastor, I have heard this from so many people and church boards: "Pastor, we need to have a revival." The problem with a revival is that people associate it with an emotional or spiritual high. It's true that this "high" may occur, but if we never look at why we are not *already* spiritually high on God, then revival will never come. If the Holy Spirit is always with me and He gives me a spirit of self-discipline, shouldn't I be able to rejoice in the Lord always, without a church service? Shouldn't I be on-fire for God all the time, since God never changes?

Rejoicing always is very difficult because of the issues of life. But I can't admit that I need revival without confessing that my spirit is experiencing death to some degree. I can't say that I need revival, while fooling myself into thinking that everything is okay. We have to admit that we are perhaps dead or at least a little comatose.

When people go to church, they want to forget their problems. They want to feel better. This is why so many preachers who always preach feel-good messages become popular. Revival comes when we cry out to God out of desperation. This desperation comes when we look at our situation honestly. We admit our weaknesses and our worries. We admit our fears and our bondage to sin. This is not something that we like to admit, especially in churches. We put on a face as if everything is okay. And we rarely criticize our own spiritual walk.

This is the same behavior the prophets of the Old Testament used to exhibit. They would point out to the Israelites where they had lost their zeal and dedication to the Lord, and call upon them to return to the Lord. Do you remember how well that went over? Well, the Israelites killed the prophets.

People do not want to hear about where their spiritual life is dead—or at best, on some kind of spiritual life support. We always want to believe that we are being faithful. We never want to look at our own sin; we would rather justify it. We don't want to admit that we have lost our zeal for the Lord. And even though we don't want to admit it, we never talk about Him outside of our church family. We have gone years or decades without leading anyone to Christ. We have stopped tithing. We haven't even invited someone to church for years.

So many of the churches in America never see even one convert over a year's time. According to the Shaeffer Institute, the number of Christians in Protestant churches from 1990 to 2000 declined by five million people, while the population grew by twenty-four million. Yet most of the Christians in the churches of America would dare to say that they love the Lord with all of their hearts. The truth is that too many churches and Christians love God like a spouse they are cheating on with another person.

We have lost sight of His standards and expectations for the believer. Does He not expect us to lead more than one person to Christ per year per church? Does He not expect that we would carry our faith and our testimony everywhere we go, in order that we would be ready to explain the glorious joy we have and the power by which we live?

Instead, we keep attending our churches, never inviting anyone else, never intentionally befriending an unbeliever for the purpose of leading him to Christ. We go to church and get the warm fuzzies in our bellies from the songs we love and the preachers who encourage us. But despite the warm fuzzies, many of us are dead and need revival. We don't need revival because we miss the spiritual highs of the past. We need revival because we have lost our zeal for God.

Revival is important. We need it. It is an essential part of our spiritual growth. If we never experience revival, our love will grow cold. We will become like many couples who wear a wedding ring but live like roommates. There is no romance or intimacy. Does this describe your walk with the living God, who gave Himself so that you might have life? Is He just some presence in your life—but nothing special?

Without revival, our relationship with God will slowly die. But how does God bring us to a place of revival? He must open our eyes to the spiritual distance between Himself and us. He is life. The more we remain in Him, the less we need revival, because every day is a fresh experience with Him. The farther we get from Him, the more death we experience, because He is life. We see ourselves fail for lack of trust or lack of purity.

So He sends us into Egypt, where He challenges our faith. He illuminates to us the places that are dead. He shows us how shallow our faith has become. He shows us how little we lean upon Him and His wisdom. When we arrive at this moment, we must repent. We *must* repent. If we do not repent, there will be no revival. Repentance brings a strange discipline from God—one in which He loves us and restores us, all the while chastising us for what we have done or refused to do.

I have experienced such grace and the revelation of God's love, and—like no other time in my life—it happens than when I am repenting for things I have done. When I fully own my sin and begin to repent and cry out to God, I am drawn nearer to Him. I pray that He will not let His Holy Spirit depart from me, just as David prayed. When I repent, I have to admit that there are areas of my life that are dead. Sin is the undeniable proof of that death.

In the midst of that cry of repentance, God appears. He does not give me excuses, and He does not sweep my sin under the rug. But He will appear with incredible love, mercy, and grace—laced with punishment and chastisement. It is this "sweet discipline," as I like to call it, that brings revival. When I am able to fully see how evil I have been, in light of this incredible forgiveness and love, I will gain a greater understanding of the depth of God's love for me. I will emerge from this process more devoted and more on-fire for the God who loves me like no other. I come forth more faithful and true to Him. I am revived.

Revival begins at the point of death. God will bring us to a place of desperation or repentance so that we might be revived. Abram was brought there by sin. We can see that Job was brought to the place of thorough desperation by his circumstances. Both are designed to create a sense of need for God. Along this journey, we will never reach our destination unless we embrace those places of desperation that come to us as a result of our sin or hardship. Our repentance or cry for help draws us closer to God. There we are revived. If we never admit our sin, we will not repent. If we remain oblivious to our problems and suffering, we will never cry out to God. Without repentance and desperation, there is no revival.

What is hindering your revival now? Is there sin in your life that is slowly killing your spirit? Are you numbing your problems with alcohol or work? Confess your sins. Cry out for help. He will come to you and you will be made alive again. This is part of the journey.

What was God's purpose in driving Abram to Egypt? God used it as a moment of circumcision to cut away the ease with which Abram released God's blessing. God used Abram's sin as a point of revival, creating in him a stronger desire to hold on to God and fight for His plans.

May our sin and trouble in this life always lead to revival. Some of us need revival now, and it is right here. We need to repent of our sins, and revival will come. We need to stop trying to do everything on our own and allow the problems we are facing to drive us to a desperation for God. Both grave sin and deep repentance are companions when we find ourselves falling into the depths of death, and they cause us to emerge into a life that is stronger, more powerful, more able to overcome, and more pure—a life filled with abundant peace. Revive us, oh Lord!

Chapter 5
Blessed Discipline

The Trespass Offering

Let's go a little bit deeper into this idea of revival. In the Old Testament, some people suffered from leprosy. Without going into the typology of leprosy, I would just say that leprosy was not only a disease that the Israelites dealt with, but it was also intended in Scripture to be a symbol of sin and death. Understanding this, we learn a lot from the process of purification for those lepers who were healed. This process mirrors for us the way the Lord wants us to work through our own sin. Let's walk through this process.

First, when a leper was diagnosed by the priest as having leprosy, he was required to remain outside the camp. This is significant and begins to reveal some of the symbolism God used. The ashes of offerings required by God in the Old Testament were taken outside the camp to a place designated for them. These ashes represented sin, and God required that they be disposed of outside the camp as a statement that sin should not be allowed within the camp of the heart. When Christ was crucified, the Scripture says that He became sin. He was crucified outside the city, just like the ashes.

God is serious about getting sin out of our hearts, minds, bodies, and souls. So those with leprosy, which also represented sin, were not allowed into the city. They had to remain outside. When a person appeared to have been healed, the priest did not call the leper to himself. Instead, the priest went outside the city. If the leprosy was gone, the former leper still was not allowed to come into the camp until the priest went through a purification process.

For this purification ceremony, the priest needed two clean, live birds, some cedar wood, scarlet yarn, and hyssop. One of the birds was killed over fresh water so that the blood flowed into the water. The priest then took the live bird, the cedar wood, the scarlet yarn, and the hyssop and dipped them into the blood. Then he sprinkled the blood onto the healed leper. He did this seven times and then released the live bird.

The priest went outside the camp and killed a live bird, and water and blood were mixed. Christ was taken outside the camp, where a soldier pierced his side, and a mixture of blood and water flowed out of his body.

The priest dipped the live bird, the cedar wood, the scarlet yarn, and the hyssop into the blood. Christ was nailed to wood and covered in blood, and a soldier offered Him hyssop while He was on the cross.

The live bird was dipped into the blood, just as we are covered by the blood of Christ. The live bird was set free, just as we who are in Christ are set free from the law of sin and death. Christ is represented by the bird who died. We are represented by the bird who is set free after being dipped into the blood of the bird who died. We are saved by the blood of Jesus Christ.

The purpose of this ceremony was to declare the leper cleansed, and it allowed him back into the camp. However, he was unable to go into his tent until a second ceremony was conducted on the eighth day. This was significant. The first ceremony allowed the leper back into the camp, but it did not allow him back to his tent, his home, or the temple for worship. The first ceremony symbolized how we are forgiven of our sin. It was a foreshadowing of how God would provide the justification for us to be forgiven.

The New Testament says that without the shedding of blood there is no forgiveness. Without Christ giving His life, we could not be forgiven. Someone who did not deserve death—which was the punishment for sin—had to receive death in our place so that we might live. We must find the faith that Jesus died for the punishment of our sin. Then we are free through faith in Him.

When we deal with our own sin, we must have faith. We must believe that we are forgiven. In fact, the Scripture says that we are the righteousness of God. In other words, God credits us with the righteousness of Christ and does not hold any of our sin against us. We must believe this, or our past sins will destroy our future blessings.

I know that some people might want to beat themselves up over atrocities they believe they have committed. But the Scripture teaches us that we are forgiven by our faith in Christ. We must force our minds, our words, and our actions to comply with this truth. If we do not force ourselves to comply, then we are saying we have faith, but we really don't. This is not a feeling. Feelings are deceptive. I am not saying that we are going to *feel* forgiven. I am saying that we must choose to believe and *live* as if we are forgiven. The feelings will come later.

"If we confess our sins, he is faithful and just and will forgive us our sins and purify us from all unrighteousness" (1 John 1:9 NIV).

I admit that many times I've gotten stuck condemning myself, but hopefully you, like me, can eventually come to a place of faith where you realize that God is faithful to forgive us. I am forgiven. You are forgiven. The only condemnation we receive after committing sin and asking for forgiveness comes from other people and from our own hearts. God does *not* condemn you if you have put your faith in Christ. "Therefore, there is now no condemnation for those who are in Christ Jesus, because through Christ Jesus the law of the Spirit of life set me free from the law of sin and death" (Romans 8:1–2 NIV).

The second ceremony for the cleansed leper came on the eighth day, and it was much more difficult to enter into than the faith represented by the first ceremony. The second part of this cleansing, which allowed the leper back into his own tent, required the priest to make a trespass offering followed by a burnt offering. These involved the sacrifice of lambs.

The purpose of a trespass offering was different from the offering of the bird in the first part of this ceremony. The first ceremony with the birds was for forgiveness, similar to our asking God to forgive us. But the purpose of a trespass offering was for the injury caused by the sin. Christ said that when we love it fulfills the law, because all biblical law leads us to act in love toward others and toward God. Obedience to God's law brings love. Disobedience brings pain, hurt, and injury. This ceremony was all about making right what sin had made wrong. It was a reminder of God's principle of restitution.

Restitution is the act of making things right. It involves doing as much as we are able to fix what we have messed up because of our sin. Asking God for forgiveness of our sins is good and must be done, but God also wants us to go to the person we sinned against and make things right. Asking forgiveness, paying for damages we caused, or working to pay off a debt we tried to skip out on are all ways of making restitution. I really think that books could and should be written about restitution. It is the part of repentance that is too often completely forgotten.

Remember that this symbolism comes from the ceremonies required for a leper to be allowed back into the camp and then into his own tent and the temple. Throughout Scripture, leprosy represents sin and death. The sting of death is sin, the Scripture tells us, so sin and death are very close cousins. Death is the scorpion in the desert, and sin is the stinger with the poison. Sin is how we know we have been touched by the spirit of death.

Both of these ceremonies had to be carried out in order for the issue of leprosy to be dealt with. Without restitution, the effects of our sin are not completely dismissed. We are forgiven, but we have created a poor witness of who God is. If we claim to be a Christian but don't love people enough to make things right, this can cause some to turn away from God. It can cause them to doubt the truth of Christianity.

Restitution reestablishes a positive feeling about God among those we have hurt. I personally believe that this is one of the biggest issues in the church. We have no problem coming to church and confessing our sins to the Lord, but God forbid that we should actually own our sin, take responsibility, and make things right as much as we can. Instead, we allow tension to remain between brothers and sisters in the Lord. We allow tension to remain between husband and wife, mother-in-law and daughter-in-law, preacher and layman. We want to be forgiven, but we don't want to do the hard work of repairing the damage we have done. And this is wrong.

When I was a youth pastor, I got myself into a little bit of trouble with the leadership of the church. I preached a message that I called, "Once Sanctified, Always Sanctified." It was a play off of a criticism I'd heard a lot in that church about brothers and sisters in Christ who followed the teachings of John Calvin and believed in eternal security. Simply stated, this belief holds that once a person sincerely gives his heart to the Lord Jesus Christ, there is no possibility of losing his salvation. Often this is referred to as "once saved, always saved."

This phrase had been used by some of the members in that church in a less than loving way. I don't agree with the teaching of John Calvin. I follow the teachings of John Wesley. However, the negative, judgmental way it was said, especially in light of the behavior of some people in that church, didn't sit well with me. These were plank-eye people. They pointed out everything they thought was wrong with everyone else, but they acted as if they themselves were perfect. Everyone knows at least one plank-eye person, but I hope to never become one.

"Why do you look at the speck of sawdust in your brother's eye and pay no attention to the plank in your own eye? How can you say to your brother, 'Let me take the speck out of your eye,' when all the time there is a plank in your own eye? You hypocrite, first take the plank out of your own eye, and then you will see clearly to remove the speck from your brother's eye" (Matthew 7:3–5 NIV).

The apostle Paul taught the doctrine of sanctification. Sanctification was often understood to mean that the sinful nature was eradicated completely. However, this teaching led to the belief in a person's ability to become so mature that they would no longer sin, because the sinful nature that makes us susceptible to sin no longer exists. This is not true.

If I have come to the point where I never sin, then I have become perfect in my ability to love. If I am perfect, I have nothing left to work on. If I always love everyone perfectly, including my enemies, then I can say that there is no sin in me. But Scripture teaches us that unless we are always increasing and maturing, we will become ineffective as Christians. Jesus taught a very sobering message about Christians who are ineffective and not producing fruit, when he cursed the fig tree that was not producing fruit. The Bible says that if we are without sin, we are liars. But I digress.

This belief about sanctification—mainly among the older generation of this particular church—was causing people to refuse to make restitution. They sinned against one another and treated others with rudeness and, at times, borderline hatred. But they never made restitution, because that would have been a form of admitting guilt or sin, which was impossible because they were "sanctified." They believed that their sinful nature had been eradicated.

But their definition of sanctification was not biblical. My message was a sarcastic commentary on the hypocrisy of those who judged Calvinists for believing that once they were saved, they were always saved—while believing of themselves that once a person was sanctified he was always sanctified and that there was no possibility of sinning. The people stuck in this belief system were dying emotionally. They were miserable—and miserable to be around.

It was really quite sad. Had they admitted that, though sanctified, they were not perfect, they could have freely asked for forgiveness and made restitution. These people needed the second ceremony that allowed the leper back into his tent and the temple and back into relationship with people and with God. Without restitution, our relationships with people and with God suffer. We must make restitution.

First, there was the sin offering and then the trespass offering. After that, the priest offered a "burnt offering." The purpose of a burnt offering was to say thank you. It was a praise offering. It was worship. The burnt offering followed the trespass offering, revealing to us that a sense of gratitude, worship, and revival follows restitution.

Let's be honest. We don't like making restitution. I don't mind asking the Lord to forgive me, but the last thing I want to do is go and ask forgiveness from someone who has offended me by their own sin. The last thing I want to do is admit my fault, my guilt before someone who might not be as gracious as God would be. However, when I am looking into the face of the person I have offended, it is a humbling experience. It is so much easier to stay in my little prayer closet and talk to a God who loves me than it is to look into the face of pain caused by my sin.

But it was the trespass offering that allowed the leper back into his tent. His tent was his home. It was the place where he could relax and be at peace. Restitution brings us peace. The purpose of the burnt offering following the trespass offering was to teach us restitution. Owning our sin and guilt—and then receiving forgiveness, along with a greater knowledge and acceptance of why we don't deserve forgiveness—produces a boundless spirit of worship and gratefulness.

As I am writing this book, I am teaching a series called, "Deliver Us from Evil." In this series, I am teaching that anything that disrupts or breaks the perfect peace and harmony of God's plan for us is evil. The first time we see evil is in the garden of Eden. The Serpent, who is the Devil, slithered into the garden and led Adam and Eve into temptation and sin. This veiled God's plan for Adam and Eve, which was embodied in the garden of Eden.

Evil is anything we do that hinders the Holy Spirit from revealing God's plan for our lives, our Eden. It is also anything we do that breaks the Eden of others. Love is the foundation of obedience to the Lord, and love never intentionally goes against the peace and harmony of God in our own lives or the lives of others. For this reason, Scripture teaches us to let nothing come out of our mouths except what is good for building others up.

Think about all those times that something came out of your mouth that did not build up, encourage, or foster the peace of God. That was sin. It was evil. Think of how many things we have done that have broken the peace of God in our own lives or the lives of others. When we consider this definition of evil, we begin to understand the apostle Paul when he said that nothing good lived in him. At first glance through worldly wisdom, this doesn't make sense. But Paul was referring to the great distance between the sin of man and the perfect holiness of God.

In our society, we justify sin and diminish it so that we don't have to own it or make restitution for it. But if I am not fully aware of my sinful state, how can I fully appreciate the love of God for a sinner like me? As long as we think of ourselves as "pretty good guys," we will never understand the greatness of God's love for us and the depth of His sacrifice. We are evil compared to the goodness of God.

Think about these words of Christ: "A certain ruler asked him, 'Good teacher, what must I do to inherit eternal life?' 'Why do you call me good?' Jesus answered. 'No one is good—except God alone'" (Luke 18:18–19 NIV).

Here we have Christ, who is God, saying that only God is good. What? That also does not make any sense. Surely, Christ Himself was good. But Jesus asked, "Why do you call me good?" If we will study this further, we find that, even though Christ was God, He became man. He was completely God and completely man at the same time. Because the nature of man had been born into Him while on the earth, He did not think it right to consider Himself good, even though He was still God.

This is a great illumination of the evil within our humanity. Not even the holiness of Christ could wipe out the evil of humanity. Christ never submitted to this evil, but the mere presence of it moved Christ to ask, "Why do you call me good?"

Because we don't have a full appreciation of the depth of our sin, we also do not have a full appreciation for the love of God, expressed in Christ's dying for the likes of us. Restitution is key in grasping the depth of our sin and enjoying the depth of His love. The burnt offering that followed the trespass offering reveals to us that greater appreciation and deeper worship follows restitution.

Through this process, we get the monkey off our back. After we have made restitution, we have done everything we can do to overcome the effects our sin. At that point, as far as it concerns us, we have done all we can do to repair our wrong. It doesn't mean we have completely fixed the situation, but it does mean that we have put forth the effort, as much as we can, to right our wrong. From this point forward, there is nothing left to keep us in bondage to that sin.

We have asked the Lord to forgive us, and He is faithful. We have asked the person we sinned against to forgive us, and we have done everything we can to fix our mess. After that, it is between the other person and their God. We are released, and God has completely restored us. How wonderful it is to know that our utmost evil is erased and we are restored.

This overwhelming joy is what Abram must have felt as he returned to Bethel. He knew he had lied. He knew how quickly he had given up God's blessing and plan for his life. He knew that what he deserved from God was not at all what he had received. He should have lost his wife. He should have lost the promise of a son. He should have lost God's plan for his life, his destiny. He should have lost his life for lying to Pharaoh. Instead, despite his great sin, God protected him. God protected his wife. God protected His plan for Abram's destiny.

The combination of asking God for forgiveness, making restitution, and understanding the evil of our sin clarifies the greatness of God's grace. It produces a spirit of thankfulness that brings revival to our souls.

Without revival, there is no destiny. So many of us want to move into God's plan for our lives, but we have not mastered the act of restitution. The moment of restitution is where the gravity of our sin and mistakes are at their height in our minds. Without this realization, the love of God is diminished. Without knowing the full measure of God's love, we will never have the confidence in God to carry us through the difficult times and tests that are necessary along our journey. We will get bogged down and stifled. We will pitch a tent and remain where we are for the rest of our lives.

Too many who have been called to greatness in God are camping out in the desert, roasting marshmallows with their faithful companion—the sin of the past. They have been called to greatness, but they are living in the tent of offense, insecurity, unforgiveness, fear, and disappointment. There is a whole nation of believers who have never come close to the glory God intended for their lives, because they have pitched a tent and refused to make restitution. Restitution is not optional. It is not just a suggestion from God. Restitution is imperative in order to continue on the journey with God so that His plans for our lives might be fulfilled.

Don't wait any longer. Call your brother. Go to your mom. Maybe they don't have any desire to see you or hear from you because of whatever may have happened. So what? Write them a letter or a Facebook message. Send them an e-mail. Leave a message on their voice mail. Do all you can do, and then let it go. Run to God with the pain it stirs. Let Him heal the brokenness that has lasted so long. Isn't it time to fold up the tent and move on? Get up. C'mon, let's go!

Blessed Discipline

Abram lied. He sinned. He walked into Egypt knowing that his wife was beautiful and would be desired by Pharaoh. He was right: Pharaoh desired her. However, rather than kill Abram, Pharaoh blessed him. Pharaoh gave Abram an enormous amount of wealth in order to take Sarai as his bride. No doubt, from a human perspective, Abram had saved his own skin.

"When Abram came to Egypt, the Egyptians saw that she was a very beautiful woman. And when Pharaoh's officials saw her, they praised her to Pharaoh, and she was taken into his palace. He treated Abram well for her sake, and Abram acquired sheep and cattle, male and female donkeys, menservants and maidservants, and camels" (Genesis 12:14–16 NIV).

Then God afflicted Pharaoh and his household with sickness and somehow communicated to Pharaoh that Abram had lied. Pharaoh called Abram before him and chastised Abram for being dishonest with him. He gave Sarai back to Abram. Then Pharaoh commanded that Abram leave with all of his possessions.

Leave with all of his possessions? Wait just a minute! When Abram entered Egypt, he was blessed already, but did he just leave Egypt *more* blessed and *more* wealthy than when he had first arrived? It looks like it! Did God just bless Abram, even though he had sinned? Is that possible? Well, apparently so!

Even though Abram had been unfaithful, God still blessed him through Pharaoh. It was God who let Pharaoh know the truth. It was God who told Pharaoh to give Sarai back. Why didn't God also command Pharaoh to take back all of the wealth he had given to Abram for Sarai? This goes against everything we have ever been taught. When we sin, there is punishment. When we sin, there is wrath. God breaks out the lightning bolts and shoots them down upon our heads. When we sin, God unleashes hell on us, and we suffer great atrocities. This is what we have always been taught. But that's not what He did with Abram.

Perhaps God just loved Abram more than He loved everyone else. Well, that can't be right, because Scripture teaches us that God is not a respecter of persons, so He does not show favoritism. It's the simple truth that God allowed Abram to be blessed—even through his sin. Definitely, God disciplined Abram. He did not simply overlook Abram's actions and act as though they had not happened. Abram knew that it was God who had revealed the truth to Pharaoh. There is no doubt that God disciplined Abram. But this was a "blessed" discipline.

From the time I was little, I've heard people speaking about the wrath of God. Perhaps it was all of the hell, fire, and brimstone preaching I was raised with. I don't know. Perhaps it was all of the Old Testament teachings saying that we should fear God. Once, when I was ministering as a chaplain to a woman whose mom was under hospice care, I asked her what her beliefs were about God. She said she was very confused, because she had always heard that we are supposed to be afraid of God. I wasn't quite sure where she was coming from at first, but as the conversation continued, she said that she could not see how a God who was to be feared could also be a God who loved unconditionally. She asked me, "Why are we supposed to be afraid of God, and why does He want us to be afraid of Him?"

These questions epitomize a huge misunderstanding about God. It is a misunderstanding that also bleeds into the perception of God's method of disciplining His children. We have been taught that we are supposed to fear God, and preachers of both the past and present have run this into the ground. I will never forget a sermon I heard during a revival only a few years ago by an "old-time" evangelist. The sermon went through the entire Bible, pointing out how many times God called for people to be killed or struck them dead instantaneously when they sinned. The intent of the message was to scare us all into heaven, I suppose. Certainly she produced a great deal of guilt in the people that day. In fact, many Christians walk around with guilt and seem to believe that God is angry with them. This absolutely does not characterize how God feels about us when we sin.

"If anyone hears my words but does not keep them, I do not judge that person. For I did not come to judge the world, but to save the world" (John 12:47 NIV). The point of God's discipline is not to make us feel condemned. On the contrary, He does not want us to feel condemned. If we have confessed our sin, and especially if we have made restitution, why should we continue to feel guilty? Why should I let my past sin seep into my thoughts every time I am in church? The Bible says that it is thrown into the sea (Micah 7:19). If you are a follower of Jesus Christ, a guilty, condemned conscience does not come from God.

> Therefore, brothers, since we have confidence to enter the Most Holy Place by the blood of Jesus, by a new and living way opened for us through the curtain, that is, his body, and since we have a great priest over the house of God, let us draw near to God with a sincere heart in full assurance of faith, having our hearts sprinkled to cleanse us from a guilty conscience and having our bodies washed with pure water. Let us hold unswervingly to the hope we profess, for he who promised is faithful. And let us consider how we may spur one another on toward love and good deeds. Let us not give up meeting together, as some are in the habit of doing, but let us encourage one another—and all the more as you see the Day approaching. (Hebrews 10:19–25 NIV)

Guilt does not help me remain true to my faith in God. Guilt challenges it. Guilt is a continued sense of *not* being right before God, of *not* being forgiven. It keeps me from moving forward with God. How can we continue to journey with God when we wonder if God is pleased with us or not?

The Bible says that we *must* believe that God wants to bless those who earnestly seek Him. Abram left everything to follow a God he could not see or touch to a place he did not know. I would say that Abram was following God earnestly, but he still sinned. If we carry around guilt from sins forgiven, it becomes difficult to have confidence that God wants to bless us, that He still loves us. It stifles us spiritually. We cannot hold unswervingly to a hope that we profess only on the outside, while we wonder on the inside what God really thinks about us. Right now, you must know that if you worship Jesus Christ as the Son of God who is risen from the grave, you are forgiven!

You are forgiven even before you sin, though God knows you are going to sin. When we sin, it does not mean that we have denied Christ as our Lord and Savior altogether. It does not mean that we have ceased to be His follower or His child. It just means that, for the moment, we have fallen victim to our sinful nature. We must understand that when we give ourselves to the Lord, we become a new creation. We don't become a new creation after every cycle of sin and forgiveness. Our state of forgiveness does not change every time we sin. God is not up in heaven with a pencil and a very good eraser, writing our names in the Book of Life and then erasing it, then writing it, then erasing it, then writing it, then … well, I think you get the idea.

Don't get me wrong. We can fall out of grace with God. Judas Iscariot did. Christ had given him power over demons. Christ never would have divided His own kingdom by giving someone who was only pretending to follow him the power to cast out demons. He would have been giving Judas an incredible platform—the inner circle of Christ's disciples—to skew the teachings of Christ. So, at one point, Judas was a sincere follower of Christ.

In the end, Judas betrayed Christ, and although he was remorseful, he never repented as Peter did, and Judas fell from grace. We know that at some point he became obsessed with money and started stealing, but at what point he fell from grace, we don't really know. It all culminated with the kiss of betrayal on the cheek of Jesus when he led the Roman soldiers to take Him into custody. But when this change happened in Judas' heart, we do not know.

We cannot take advantage of God's grace and continue to sin. If we continue to sin, we will fall out of grace. This does not mean that we will someday become perfect, but rather that we are gaining maturity. If I continue to commit the same sins I committed a long time ago, am I really growing in my spiritual maturity? Of course not. Living by the Holy Spirit will produce in me a maturity that leads me away from the sins of the past. I will never be perfect, but sincerely following Christ will produce in me a spiritual maturity over the years.

Though it is possible to fall from grace, there is a huge amount of grace given to us when we sin. God's discipline is not intended to beat us down. There is no condemnation in God's discipline. God will condemn the act and the behavior, but even as He does this, He makes sure we know that He loves us.

"Therefore, there is now no condemnation for those who are in Christ Jesus, because through Christ Jesus the law of the Spirit of life set me free from the law of sin and death" (Romans 8:1–2 NIV). These are the words of the apostle Paul right after he related the struggle of sin. He said that he still committed the sin he did not want to commit and that he did not live in the righteousness he desired to. He was speaking about the battle within believers between the Holy Spirit that has come into us and the sinful nature that was born into us. If we are sincere in following Christ, our sin does not push us out of His grace, love, and blessing. If we understand and receive God's discipline, our sin does not steer us off-course in God's plan for our life. On the contrary, it anchors us into the very destiny God planned for us before the beginning of time.

God is *never* surprised by your sin. When you lie or cheat or lust or sin in your anger (or whatever), God's jaw doesn't drop in amazement. He doesn't faint from the shock. He knows. He has always known. He knows today your sins of tomorrow and the next day and next week and next year. Therefore, there is a difference between God's discipline and His condemnation. He condemns those who are obstinate and openly rebellious toward Him.

Now one of the Pharisees invited Jesus to have dinner with him, so he went to the Pharisee's house and reclined at the table. When a woman who had lived a sinful life in that town learned that Jesus was eating at the Pharisee's house, she brought an alabaster jar of perfume, and as she stood behind him at his feet weeping, she began to wet his feet with her tears. Then she wiped them with her hair, kissed them and poured perfume on them.

When the Pharisee who had invited him saw this, he said to himself, "If this man were a prophet, he would know who is touching him and what kind of woman she is—that she is a sinner."

Jesus answered him, "Simon, I have something to tell you."

"Tell me, teacher," he said.

"Two men owed money to a certain moneylender. One owed him five hundred denarii, and the other fifty. Neither of them had the money to pay him back, so he canceled the debts of both. Now which of them will love him more?"

Simon replied, "I suppose the one who had the bigger debt canceled."

"You have judged correctly," Jesus said.

Then he turned toward the woman and said to Simon, "Do you see this woman? I came into your house. You did not give me any water for my feet, but she wet my feet with her tears and wiped them with her hair. You did not give me a kiss, but this woman, from the time I entered, has not stopped kissing my feet. You did not put oil on my head, but she has poured perfume on my feet. Therefore, I tell you, her many sins have been forgiven—for she loved much. But he who has been forgiven little loves little."

Then Jesus said to her, "Your sins are forgiven."

The other guests began to say among themselves, "Who is this who even forgives sins?"

Jesus said to the woman, "Your faith has saved you; go in peace." (Luke 7:36–50 NIV)

In this moment, we see God's discipline. This woman was sinful, full of sin. She had engaged in the things of the flesh, not of the spirit. But she had heard about this man Jesus. She believed Him to be the Messiah, sent from God. Yet she did not have the impression from what she had heard about Him—or from his own lips—that she would be condemned if she went into His presence. Not only did she *not* feel that she would be condemned, but what she had learned about Jesus actually *moved* her into His presence. She wept. She worshipped. She did not care what anyone thought. To be in the presence of Jesus, this sinful woman risked her life by coming into a Pharisee's home.

Christ received her and protected her—even as He told a parable that indicated indirectly that this woman had sinned much. This must have stung, as she realized that He was speaking of her great sin. He did not overlook it or gloss over it. He dealt with it. Then He moved past it and approved of her as one who loved much.

Christ was also disciplining this Pharisee. We don't know much about him, except that he invited Jesus into his home and they were reclining together. In other Scripture, we read about Pharisees who tried to trap Jesus in His own words, and He condemned them. But this Pharisee was treated differently. He was disciplined gently, in a way that pointed out the grace of God toward the sinful woman, while reproving the Pharisee for not loving as he should because of the arrogance in his own heart.

Jesus did not call this Pharisee a whitewashed tomb or a viper, as He did with other Pharisees. This Pharisee was not trying to trap Jesus. He had invited Jesus over with sincere intentions, but God's love proved to be more than what he understood. Because this Pharisee was attempting to be sincere, I believe, it caused Christ to be more gentle with him than with other religious leaders of the time. This Pharisee did not honor Christ as He should have, but he was not against Christ, as much as he was conflicted by Christ. He was confused by what he had been taught about the Messiah and what he had seen in the person of Jesus Christ.

Jesus was gentle. He is a gentle disciplinarian for those who are sincerely trying to work through their sinful tendencies to worship Him in spirit and truth.

On the other hand, here is a Scripture where we see Christ condemning Pharisees whose intentions were not to find God but to build up their own reputations:

> "Woe to you, teachers of the law and Pharisees, you hypocrites! You clean the outside of the cup and dish, but inside they are full of greed and self-indulgence. Blind Pharisee! First clean the inside of the cup and dish, and then the outside also will be clean. Woe to you, teachers of the law and Pharisees, you hypocrites! You are like whitewashed tombs, which look beautiful on the outside but on the inside are full of dead men's bones and everything unclean. In the same way, on the outside you appear to people as righteous but on the inside you are full of hypocrisy and wickedness. Woe to you, teachers of the law and Pharisees, you hypocrites! You build tombs for the prophets and decorate the graves of the righteous. And you say, 'If we had lived in the days of our forefathers, we would not have taken part with them in shedding the blood of the prophets.' So you testify against yourselves that you are the descendants of those who murdered the prophets. Fill up, then, the measure of the sin of your forefathers! You snakes! You brood of vipers! How will you escape being condemned to hell?" (Matthew 23:25–33 NIV)

Do you hear the different tone in His voice? These Pharisees were those who walked around with Scriptures on their foreheads and arms so that they were always memorizing Scripture. They were teachers of the Law, but Christ knew their hearts. He knew that despite their outward righteousness, their hearts were far from loving God. Christ condemned the insincere Pharisees.

On the other hand, the sinful woman was sincere. She had come to a place of repentance, and Christ approved of her and used her as an example of someone who learned to love Him much. The sinful woman and Simon the Pharisee were each given gentle discipline intended to draw them closer to God. Christ had the same purpose for both His gentle, blessed discipline of Simon and the woman and His harsh discipline of the rebellious Pharisees. Both the gentle discipline and the condemning discipline were based in love. God does nothing outside of love.

But those who were insincere needed to be condemned in this way to open their eyes, to break their pride. They were so convinced of their own righteousness that they denied their sin, promoted their spirituality, and felt deserving of God's goodness.

The woman did not think too highly of herself. She was not prideful. She was aware of and remorseful for her sin. She owned it and hated it. By coming to Christ, her remorse led her to repentance and the desire and determination to do better. She received a blessed discipline. She left that moment of discipline not condemned but blessed.

To continue our journey with God, it is imperative that we know and understand the difference between God's discipline for believers and His discipline for unbelievers. If you are sincere in following Christ, there will be a humility in you. You will be very aware of the sin in you. You will be repentant, desiring with all of your heart to never return to that sin. There will be a sense of unworthiness before the presence of God, instead of a sense of entitlement to God's blessings. One is like the child who is sent to his room with a tone of disappointment from his father. The other is like the child who is kicked out of the house because of sustained rebellion and a lack of effort to submit to his father's authority.

Those who truly want to follow Christ but mess up will be treated with a gentle and even blessed discipline. Those who are playing games with

God, pretending to love Him while continuing in their sin, will be condemned. When Abram left Egypt, he had been reproved. He had been chastised. There had been discipline, no doubt. But it was a blessed discipline, and he left Egypt with a greater appreciation for God's grace. This grace gave him strength in his spirit to remain and continue with God. He did not leave with so much guilt and condemnation that he fell away. He left humbled … and blessed.

Now the question for you and me is this: if God's discipline is gentle and blessed, why do we still condemn ourselves? Zombies are those who are dead but who walk around as if they are alive. Christians who condemn themselves are spiritual zombies. They are alive, but they walk around as if they are dead.

As we have already seen, sin is represented by leprosy in the Old Testament. God is trying to help us understand sin through the symbol of a disease. He sees sin as a disease. This is why Jesus did so much healing. It was a symbol of what He wants to do in our spirits. He wants to heal us of the inherited, sinful nature in us.

For this reason, the apostle Paul urged us to live by the Spirit. It is not that we are healed, but we are in the process of being healed, so we are to live by the Spirit. Don't disconnect from the IV that is feeding your spirit the healing medicine it needs. Live by the Spirit. Stay connected. Have you ever seen a doctor come into a room and beat the tar out of a patient for being sick? No, of course not! Jesus is the Great Physician. He is in the process of healing those who follow Him, and cleansing them from unrighteousness. He is not surprised that you show symptoms of the disease of sin. When you have faith, He credits you with righteousness, though you are not righteous on your own. Then He begins to cleanse you of your unrighteous behavior through the power and teaching of the Holy Spirit and the Word of God. And He does not give up on you when you mess up.

Confess your sin. Make restitution. Accept His forgiveness and continue on the journey with Him. Be blessed, even in His discipline.

Mistakes and Sin

I have to stop here and take note of something spectacular. Let's consider for just a moment that God is omniscient. There is nothing He does not know. He has known every day of history from the first day until the last day, which has yet to appear. He has known each day of your life from the moment you were conceived until the time you will finally pass into the next realm. More than this, He knows what is going to happen to you each day. He even knows what you are going to do each day. He knows the good deeds you will do. He knows every sin you will commit. He knows every mistake that you will make throughout your entire lifetime. He knows the good decisions and the bad. He knows every thought and every idea. He is all-knowing.

When Abram walked into Egypt, God knew what was going to happen. God was fully aware that this experience was going to test Abraham and that he would fail the test. He knew that Abram would be afraid. God knew that he would lie. He knew it all. God is never surprised by anything.

And yet God caused Pharaoh to look favorably toward Abram so that when Pharaoh took Sarai, he gave Abram a great deal of wealth. This was customary, but keep in mind that Abram was just a foreigner coming through Pharaoh's territory. Even though giving wealth was customary, some monarchs, especially back then, could have brutally murdered Abram or given him nothing for Sarai. Instead, Pharaoh gave great wealth to Abram. God's favor was upon Abram, even though He knew Abram was going to fail this test and sin. He knew it, and yet His favor remained.

Wow! Is that not amazing? Why would God do this? Why would He maintain blessings upon Abram? God knew that Abram was going to make a huge mistake in that moment, but He also knew that Abram was still going to work to follow God the rest of his life. Abram was sincere. He was not fake, not playing games with God. He truly desired to serve God wholeheartedly. He just failed.

Have you ever failed or made a huge mistake? It is so easy to carry around this grand regret that taints every blessing from that moment on. Regret and sorrow can imprison us as much as anything in our lives. It weighs us down. Depression, regret, and sorrow form an evil trio that causes the living to die on the inside, in their spirits. This trio is competent in its wicked craft.

Consider this Scripture: "Godly sorrow brings repentance that leads to salvation and leaves no regret, but worldly sorrow brings death" (2 Corinthians 7:10 NIV). The Scripture teaches us that there are two sorrows: a worldly sorrow that brings death and a godly sorrow that brings repentance. Godly sorrow leads to salvation and leaves no regret.

How can the great mistakes—or even worse, great sins—of our past leave no regret? If we can learn to process our regret and sorrow through God's eyes, they will lead us back to God. In the presence of God, we find forgiveness. There, we are taught. There, we set our minds to never do these things again. And there we experience the love of God at a very deep level. Sometimes we are so sure that God is angry with us or hates us or is punishing us that it is impossible to imagine otherwise.

I say again, "Therefore, there is now no condemnation for those who are in Christ Jesus." We cannot lose sight of the fact that God used all of Abram's mistakes and sin to accomplish His plan in Abram's life. God used the drought, Egypt, and Pharaoh to lead Abram back to God. Abram finished this episode back with God, because God never left him. In fact, He blessed him. God was applying pressure to Abram so he would be able to see his breaking point and know where he needed to strengthen his faith.

God allowed all of this, not that Abram would be destroyed but that he would be made fully aware of how much he needed God. God used Abram's failure to illuminate for him just how vast the love of God is. Abram's sorrow and regret led him deeper into the thick love of God. This brought revival. God knew that Abram was going to mess everything up, but in His foreknowledge, He arranged for Abram to be blessed. These blessings were important to Abram's continued walk with Christ.

We are so certain of God's displeasure with us when we sin, but God has arranged every day of our lives to teach us the lessons we need. He even teaches us through our sin and mistakes. Don't get me wrong. God hates sin. But He does not hate *you*!

During the summer of my junior year in high school, I felt a call from God to preach. After a time of wrestling with the idea, it became clear and definite to me. There was not a question in my mind. I did not walk around wondering if God was calling me or not. The idea was scorched deep into the recesses of my mind, and I knew that I was supposed to preach.

But football, oh that glorious football! (I hope you hear my sarcasm.) Football began to mess with my mind. I played fairly well during my senior year in high school, and I desired to play football in college, so I said no to preaching. I did not turn away from God, but my spiritual fervor faltered. I thought that once I said no to the call to preach, it was a done deal. I thought I had put to death this call because of my decision to tell God no.

I would later open my eyes and go into the ministry. However, during my rebellion to the call, God placed in my heart a desire to be a coach and a teacher. I had messed up. I had sinned against God. I had destroyed God's plan for my life. At least it seemed that way.

In studying to become a teacher, I took many classes that taught interpersonal skills. I learned how to better understand people and myself. Had I gone to seminary, I would not have learned these same kinds of truths. I would have learned more about the Bible, but I would not have learned so much about how to interact with people and how to teach in a way that kept people engaged and presented the subject matter clearly at the same time.

I also met my wife at college. She has been the perfect wife for me. She has been so instrumental in my spiritual maturity. I know that God used my saying no to Him to bring me to a place of blessing. I learned things I never would have learned without this time of rebellion. It's crazy. How wonderful is our God!

God knows what sins you have committed and what sins you will commit. He is not surprised. In His foreknowledge, He has arranged to work around the sin you have committed or that you are going to commit. He knows that, although you are going to sin, your heart is still trying its best to follow Him. He uses our sins and our mistakes to bring us into His journey for our lives. He only does this if we take the sorrow we experience from our sins and mistakes to Him, where He comforts His child. If we use our sorrow as an excuse to leave the presence of God and never return to Him, we will forever lose our peace. Death will follow.

Carry the sorrow of your sin to Him. Ask for forgiveness. Pray for those you have hurt. Make restitution. This is repentance. The original language for *repentance* comes from another word that is translated "no regret." Though our sins or mistakes are huge, God will use them to keep us on the journey. Though they are evil, He will use them for good. Let us strive to live with no regret and no sorrow.

Change your perception. Peter and Judas both betrayed Christ, but Peter's perception was that God still loved him and would keep loving him. After Peter's denial of Christ, we see Peter back with the men of the church. Later, we see Peter in charge of the church.

Judas, on the other hand, did not go to God for forgiveness. Instead, he went to the Pharisees to try to fix it. We can't fix it. We must stop trying to fix it. It happened. It's out there. There is nothing we can do about it. We must let it go. Judas' perception was that there was no forgiveness for him from God. He took his sorrow to a noose and hung himself.

Do not let sorrow from the past destroy you. Take your pain to God, and He will use the intimacy of sincere repentance to draw you back into His plan for your life. Then you will live with no regret, no remorse, and no sorrow!

Chapter 6
Learning to Wait

What in the World?

> After this, the word of the Lord came to Abram in a vision: "Do not be afraid, Abram. I am your shield, your very great reward."
>
> But Abram said, "O Sovereign Lord, what can you give me since I remain childless and the one who will inherit my estate is Eliezer of Damascus?" And Abram said, "You have given me no children; so a servant in my household will be my heir."
>
> Then the word of the Lord came to him: "This man will not be your heir, but a son coming from your own body will be your heir." He took him outside and said, "Look up at the heavens and count the stars—if indeed you can count them." Then he said to him, "So shall your offspring be."
>
> Abram believed the Lord, and he credited it to him as righteousness. He also said to him, "I am the Lord, who brought you out of Ur of the Chaldeans to give you this land to take possession of it."
>
> But Abram said, "O Sovereign Lord, how can I know that I will gain possession of it?" (Genesis 15:1–8 NIV)

It had been some time since God had first approached Abram to tell him that He would make him into a great nation, but Abram still didn't have a child. Abram wondered what in the world was going on. Was God not going to honor him and keep His promise? Was the deceit he had employed in Egypt so great that he had forfeited this great promise? God had done a lot of talking, but nothing was happening.

What do we do when God doesn't fulfill His part of the bargain? Confusion sets in, and confusion is dangerous. It tears at our faith. It opens us up to thoughts of doubt and worry. Abram tried to believe, but he did not have much of a reason to believe. God had simply not done what He'd said He would.

God says that He will supply all of our needs according to His riches in glory, but sometimes we go hungry. This is confusing. God says that He is our Prince of Peace and that He gives a peace that surpasses all understanding, but we don't always see intervention from God that would calm our hearts. This is confusing. Jesus said that He has come to give us life more abundantly, but sometimes everything still falls apart. This is confusing. When will He do what He says He will? Why is He holding back? How long must we wait, oh God? We cry out to God, but it seems as if the heavens have been shut up and God has turned a deaf ear to our cries. This is confusing.

As much as we hate confusion, it is part of the journey. In fact, it is essential. I know it seems strange that a God of order allows chaos to flow into our lives, but He does just that. There are times when the promises seem so far away. He just doesn't show up. He just doesn't protect. He just doesn't provide. We feel like Job, wondering where God could be. We sit there and scrape our sores, wondering when and if God is ever going to show up.

If we are not comfortable with this confusion, it will lead us down a path of doubt and questioning. We must learn to be comfortable with confusion. God doesn't do things the way we want Him to, and what He does do is so far above us that it rarely makes any sense. His ways are higher than ours (Isaiah 55:9). If we are not prepared for this confusion, divorce happens, temptations are easier to partake in, faith falters, and strength fails.

When I was first called to be a preacher, I felt something in my spirit, but I wrestled with whether or not this was what God wanted for me. When I am preparing grooms and brides for their weddings, they ask me, "How can I know that this person is the right person for me?"

We must understand this confusion and allow it to draw us closer to God, not scatter us from His presence. But how can we know what God wants of us?

What a great question to ask Him!

God seems to give great and wonderful promises and high visions, and then it seems as if nothing is happening. Absolutely nothing reveals to us concretely what God is doing or saying. "How can I know?" we ask. And He responds with silence.

I believe that one of the strangest things in Scripture is the account of some writing on the wall.

> King Belshazzar gave a great banquet for a thousand of his nobles and drank wine with them. While Belshazzar was drinking his wine, he gave orders to bring in the gold and silver goblets that Nebuchadnezzar his father had taken from the temple in Jerusalem, so that the king and his nobles, his wives and his concubines might drink from them. So they brought in the gold goblets that had been taken from the temple of God in Jerusalem, and the king and his nobles, his wives and his concubines drank from them. As they drank the wine, they praised the gods of gold and silver, of bronze, iron, wood and stone. Suddenly the fingers of a human hand appeared and wrote on the plaster of the wall, near the lampstand in the royal palace. The king watched the hand as it wrote. His face turned pale and he was so frightened that his knees knocked together and his legs gave way. (Daniel 5:1–6 NIV)

Of course, this would have freaked me out as well. I am quite sure that in reality I never want to see a human hand appear out of nowhere and start writing me a note. But part of me wishes at times that God would just send a hand down to pull a Post-it Note off my desk and start writing. It could just be a short essay entitled "Here Is What I'm Doing"—signed, God.

I could read this note and know exactly what was going on. There would be no more stress or worry. I would not be afraid or tempted to give up. I would know, and I would be content. I have been chastised by God at times. I knew that God was trying to teach me something, but I had no idea what it was. I wanted to say to God, "If you would just tell me what You are doing and what I need to learn, I would do it." Then I could relax. I would have peace. But there is no hand. There is no clue. There is no voice. There is no revelation.

If you are in the middle of great confusion after putting so much faith in God, don't be afraid. Don't stress. (This is easier for me to write than for you to do, I know.) Don't let this be a time of losing faith and losing strength. Don't you dare walk away from God just because you haven't heard from Him or seen Him in a while, for He is your very great reward. Your reward is not what He is doing or what He is going to do. His reward is not a physical blessing. It is not a job. It is not a baby. It is not a husband. *He* is your reward. And He is always with you. *You don't have to know what He is doing, as long as You know that He is with you.*

This is what Abram tells God in the middle of his confusion. "I know You have been good to me, God. I see the blessings that have come from Your hand. You have been good to me, but right now there is a storm, and You don't seem to care. I am confused."

That might be how our own prayer begins, but what about a better ending? Try, "Nevertheless, Lord, You are my very great reward. If I have you, I don't need anything else." If we let the confusion get the best of us, we are no different from the Israelites who got tired of waiting for Moses to come back down from the mountain. They said to

151

one another that Moses had been taking too long, and they were just going to eat all of his food and make their own god. They said to one another, "We need a god, so let's throw all of our gold into the oven and make for ourselves a golden calf to worship and dance around."

This is what happens when we get tired of waiting. We make a cow of golden knowledge and try to figure everything out ourselves. We start making decisions that typically do not follow God's plan. We make a cow of golden revelry, give up on God altogether, and run from Him in rebellion to partake in things we ought to be ashamed of. We throw our friends, girlfriends, boyfriends, and spouses into the fire, and out pops the god of comfort in the bed of fornication and adultery. The comfort, peace, and strength God intends for us, we begin to seek from other things and other people. God may use a spouse, a child, a mom, or a coworker to provide the comfort and company we need, but when He sends them to us, and there is no sin involved.

"I know God put him in my life. He is so good to me." This is what some women have said to me about the men they left their husbands for. I respond to them, "No, I don't think so." They come back and say, "He is so caring. He loves me." I retort, "Not even a little bit."

God will never supply our emotional needs—or any other kind of need—by providing a temptation to sin. God will not comfort you when your marriage is difficult by sending you a man who wants to have sex with you. *God does not do that!* He doesn't supply for your financial needs by giving you a job that doesn't allow you to go to church. He doesn't help you calm down by drinking margaritas with your friends until you are drunk.

God supplies your needs according to His riches in glory, not the cesspools of this world. Stay away from the golden gods of this world. They are only distractions, refractions, and reactions to the confusion we feel when we don't understand what God is doing at the moment.

This time of confusion and waiting is part of God's plan. His plan for you is not a destination, a particular job, a husband, 2.3 kids, and a two-car garage. His plan for you may work through all of these different situations, but His plan for your life is to make you into a man or woman of God who has such faith that He can easily bless you in extraordinary ways. Part of this process is for us to learn to love God, not just what He does for us. He is a person. He desires a relationship.

If the only time I went to see my rich uncle was when I needed money, he would realize after a while that I am attached more to his money than to him. God doesn't want to be taken advantage of. He won't be made a fool. Therefore, these are times when God is seeing if you are content with Him and Him alone—instead of what He can do for you. It is not that He is trying to be selfish or narcissistic. But He does know that unless you worship Him and not His blessings, your faith in Him as Savior is not sincere. He knows that unless you love Him above all things, your destiny is a dark hell.

So, He withholds blessings and understanding to give us an opportunity to love Him just for Himself. He is our very great reward. If He never blessed us again for even one second of one day for the rest of our lives, the blessings He has already given to us are enough. *He* is enough. Just knowing that God is with me is more than enough. He is our very great reward! Just sit tight and wait for God to show you the next step. Every day that you maintain your faith as you wait for Him, He causes your faith in Him, your commitment to Him, and thus your love for Him to grow more and more.

Whenever God has not shown up to answer any of my prayers or fulfill my dreams for two weeks or two months or two years, and I keep believing and loving Him, my love for Him is proved out. When I become angry or impatient with God because He has not shown up, my self-love is proved out. We need these times of confusion in order to evaluate our reactions. It is only then that we can know the sincerity of our love.

The situation will not last. God will not be silent forever. Keep believing. This confusion has come, and it will go away—and then it will come again. But during these times, love Him anyway. Because you have set your priorities straight, times of confusion prepare you for greater plans and blessings later. He is enough. He is your very great reward.

I love to go out on dates with my wife. I enjoy going to dinner, going to the movies, playing miniature golf, and so on. But one of my favorite parts of the date is being all alone with her, without distraction, holding hands. Sometimes we talk. Sometimes we don't. It doesn't matter. I love the romance of just being together. In the same way, God was about to turn Abram's moment of confusion into a very tender moment, and Abram would walk away from this confusion more dedicated and sure of his relationship with God.

When you are confused, God just wants to be with you. He just wants to sit together. Talk. Don't talk. It doesn't matter. It is the tenderness of the moment, the romance, the intimacy that will draw you to Him. You will walk away with a much greater understanding of the depth of His *love* rather than His blessings, protection, provision, vision, and dreams. His presence alone will strengthen you. He is enough. He is your very great reward.

> Hast thou not known? hast thou not heard, that the everlasting God, the Lord, the Creator of the ends of the earth, fainteth not, neither is weary? There is no searching of his understanding. He giveth power to the faint; and to them that have no might he increaseth strength. Even the youths shall faint and be weary, and the young men shall utterly fall: but they that wait upon the Lord shall renew their strength; they shall mount up with wings as eagles; they shall run, and not be weary; and they shall walk, and not faint. (Isaiah 40:28–31 KJV)

Waiting

Is there anyone who enjoys waiting? Whether you are waiting at Walmart or waiting for your wife to get ready or waiting for your husband to finally take out the trash, no one enjoys waiting. But I must say that no one makes the most of a period of waiting like God does. Waiting is definitely a test. It tests our patience and our loyalty. It tests our love and our mercy. Waiting is not for the weak.

God establishes many times of waiting in His relationship with us. We pray for things to change, and the Lord asks us to wait. We ask for answers, and we wait. We go to church. We read the Bible. We pray. We do everything that we know how to do and ask the Lord every which way we can think of. We will even ask others to ask God for us. We ask God to tell us what to do or where to go, to tell us if we need to turn around and go back. We just want Him to tell us *something*.

But often the Lord's only response is: "Wait." The difficulty of waiting is essential on our journey with God, and yet, like blessings and suffering, waiting is dangerous if we do not know how to process these periods of waiting upon the Lord. We are tempted to turn to our own thoughts, and if we turn to our own thoughts, we will certainly lose our patience and turn to other gods, other people, and other wisdom.

Waiting produces confusion. Waiting is necessary, but it is confusing. The waiting time is when we are able to see for ourselves where we stand in our faith and devotion to the Lord. Will we continue to worship Him, even though He does nothing and makes us wait? Or will we turn to other gods?

It is not that God needs to discover what is in our hearts. He already knows. This is a time of self-discovery. The reactions we have while waiting upon the Lord reveal our level of faith. They tells us how much we truly love God or how much we see God as some kind of sugar daddy. Reverence or disrespect will be found in us. We will either maintain our belief that He is God and we are not and that He can do whatever He wants—or we will deny Him as God. If we maintain that He is God, *our* God, then we will release control of our lives. Our timetable for answered prayers, blessings, and miracles will be relinquished. We will concede that every good and perfect gift can only come from God. Therefore, if He wants to wait a while before He does anything, we will be content to wait. Otherwise, we will take Him for granted, as if He is a genie that we can call out of the bottle any time we like, to do whatever we ask.

The waiting time is a mirror in front of our souls, revealing what we really look like. Sure, God could just tell us. He could just say, "Hey, you are taking advantage of me! I'm not a genie!" But let's be truthful. Would we believe Him? Would we listen? There have probably been people in our lives who have told us the same thing, and we did not listen to them either—or, at least, I didn't. I am amazed at how well we can fool ourselves and lie to ourselves and then believe our own lies. King David, a very godly man, was a great example of this.

King David took Bathsheba as his wife, because she was pregnant and her husband had tragically died at war. This was the lie that David told to himself. He never allowed the truth to surface in his own mind. He convinced himself that he was such a good king to look out for this poor widow woman. He had completely repressed any memories of seducing this woman. It just completely slipped his mind that he had sent her husband to the front of the battle to ensure his death. He just didn't remember those things.

It's incredible. It's unbelievable. And yet we do this kind of thing all the time. The Lord puts someone into our lives—such as a spouse or a friend—who attempts to bring some reality into our mind or to identify some areas that we could work on improving. But instead of accepting the input, we are offended and start pointing out everything wrong with that person. Criticism is difficult to take, even if it is constructive criticism from someone who loves us. Really, the Bible is constructive criticism from God, who loves us. But look at how many times we justify ourselves in our own minds to disobey or disregard Scripture.

We drastically underestimate the evil that would be within us if we didn't have the Holy Spirit. Without the Holy Spirit, we wouldn't even feel guilt for sin, because sin is natural. Just as we don't feel guilty about taking a breath, we would not feel guilty about committing a sin, no matter whom we may harm. That is just the truth about us and our depravity. It's why it is called a sinful *nature*. Sin is natural to us.

But the Holy Spirit is the Spirit of truth, and He lives in us. Therefore, we will always see ourselves and others in His perfect light. We will easily see our faults. We will quickly accept them without offense and will work to make them better. It will always rain but never storm. We will never hit another red light going through town. Mosquitoes will never bite. Weeds will never spring up. Ice cream will be calorie-free, and our breath will never stink … *Yeah, right!* We are too easily offended. Even with the Holy Spirit alive within us, we can lie so well to ourselves.

God is not rude in making us wait so that we can see for ourselves the true state of our faith. He is not judgmental. He is not mean. He is also not ignoring us. Instead, He is loving. Rather than beat us over the head with our faults, mistakes, and sins, He just tells us to wait. And the longer we wait, the more clearly we see who we really are. If we can continue to remain faithful to God without bitterness, anger, stress, or doubt, then each day we will see a greater level of faith. If I am praying for healing and God doesn't do it, it still took faith to pray that prayer. To continue to pray for healing every day when God does not heal requires more faith.

The waiting, when handled in a godly way, forces us to increase our own faith. It takes more faith to pray for healing after years of praying without an answer from the Lord than it takes when the diagnosis is first made. But if I fall into the temptations that accompany waiting, I will become confused and angry. I will do just as the Israelites did and turn to other gods. I will begin to act upon my own wisdom rather than God's. I will act upon my own desire instead of God's. I will do what I want instead of what God wants.

If God has brought you to a place of waiting, stop fighting it. Let go of the anger. Stop listening to your own voice or the voice of others, and listen for the voice of God, even though He may not be acting on your behalf at the moment. Perhaps He is not giving you an answer, but He is speaking. He is using this waiting time for you to see the strength or weakness of your faith, and He is saying something.

Do you hear Him? It is a still, quiet voice, but He is speaking. Turn down the anger. Tune out the anxiousness and worry. Filter out the complaining and confusion. What a great message He has for you during this time, but you must listen. His whispers are moving through your ear: "I have not forgotten you."

Chapter 7

A Covenant People

How Can I Know?

> But Abram said, "O Sovereign Lord, how can I know that I will gain possession of it?" So the Lord said to him, "Bring me a heifer, a goat and a ram, each three years old, along with a dove and a young pigeon." Abram brought all these to him, cut them in two and arranged the halves opposite each other; the birds, however, he did not cut in half. Then birds of prey came down on the carcasses, but Abram drove them away. As the sun was setting, Abram fell into a deep sleep, and a thick and dreadful darkness came over him. (Genesis 15:8–12 NIV)

Abram says to the Lord, "How can I know?" And God answered Abram. He told Abram, "Bring me a heifer. It's time for a covenant." When Abram asked God how he could know that God would keep His promise, God's answer was to make a covenant with Abram. Today, this covenant is still God's answer to us. This covenant is a promise to us that God will do His part to make His great and wonderful plans come to pass in our lives.

In Abram's day, when two men wanted to make a covenant with one another, they would take sacrificial animals and cut them in half. They separated the animal halves, creating a walkway between them—a path between the bloody pieces. Then they joined hands as they walked this path together. The symbolism of the covenant was a declaration from each party, saying, "May I be cut into pieces, just like these animals, should I not fulfill my part of the covenant." This was a blood covenant.

A covenant is different from a promise. If I promise to do something for you, then that is a promise that is not built upon anything else. No matter what may happen, I am obligated to keep my promise. However, a covenant is a promise made by two people, and each one's promise hinges on the other keeping his promise. Once one person breaks the covenant, the other is no longer bound to keep his part. It's an "if/then" promise. "If you do this, then I will do that, but if you do not do this, then I will not do that."

God made a blood covenant with Abram. He called for the sacrificial animals. Abram's part was to gather the sacrifices and prepare them. Abram created the walkway. After he had finished preparing the sacrifices and laying them out, God put Abram to sleep. This was significant. How could Abram walk through the blood if he was asleep? God made an "if/then" promise with Abram, but He did it without Abram. Abram did not take part in the symbolic walk. Instead, God put Abram to sleep and then did something that hits at the heart of Christianity. It is the underpinning of everything we know as believers of Jesus Christ.

> Then the Lord said to him, "Know for certain that your descendants will be strangers in a country not their own, and they will be enslaved and mistreated four hundred years. But I will punish the nation they serve as slaves, and afterward they will come out with great possessions. You, however, will go to your fathers in peace and be buried at a good old age. In the fourth generation your descendants will come back here, for the sin of the Amorites has not yet reached its full measure."
> When the sun had set and darkness had fallen, a smoking firepot with a blazing torch appeared and passed between the pieces. On that day the Lord made a covenant with Abram and said, "To your descendants I give this land, from the river of Egypt to the great river, the Euphrates—the land of the Kenites, Kenizzites, Kadmonites, Hittites, Perizzites, Rephaites, Amorites, Canaanites, Girgashites and Jebusites." (Genesis 15:13–21 NIV)

This was God's answer to Abram's question, "How can I know?" God's answer was a blood covenant, but neither God nor Abram walked through the blood. Instead, a smoking firepot and a blazing torch appeared. These went through the blood as two men would have done.

The blazing torch was from God to represent Himself. He is the Light. He is the fire. Later we see God in the form of a burning bush, a fire. The Holy Spirit is identified as fire. We are told in the New Testament that we will be baptized by water and by fire, which refers to the Holy Spirit. Jesus would call Himself the Light, and He calls us to walk in that Light. This blazing torch was God's representation of Himself as the fire and the Light. He did not represent Himself as a small fire but as a blazing torch. He is strong. He is powerful. We don't ever need to wonder about the power of God. If He says that He will do something, He keeps His promise, and He is able—more than able—to do whatever He chooses. "But the plans of the Lord stand firm forever, the purposes of his heart through all generations" (Psalm 33:11 NIV).

The other object that miraculously appeared was a smoking firepot. The firepot went through the blood along with the blazing torch. The firepot represented Abram. The firepot was smoking because it had been heated with fire. Firepots were conduits of the fire. Fire was put in them and was maintained in them.

When we receive Jesus Christ as our Lord and Savior, we are given the Holy Spirit, the fire of God, to remain in us. This fire is the Spirit of truth, the Counselor who helps us in our journey with God. The smoke was there, because the firepot contained the fire of God, just as the holy fire of God resides in our hearts. This firepot represented Abram as the one in whom God's spirit was, but it also represents every believer, as we also are the firepot in which the Holy Spirit, the fire, dwells.

But Abram was right there, sleeping. Why didn't God send Abram through? Why did God choose to create His own firepot instead of having Abram walk through? God had put Abram to sleep, almost as if He wanted Abram to rest as the covenant was being established.

Jesus Christ was God, manifested as a man. Though He was God, He was a man, and He chose to live life on earth as a man. He did not live as God. The firepot represented man. Just as the firepot was miraculously produced by the hand of God, so Christ was immaculately conceived in the womb of a virgin. He came to live as a man so that He might die as a man.

Later, we will see that the first Passover in Moses' time required that the Israelites bring forth a "perfect" lamb, without blemish, for sacrifice. Jesus Christ had to be a perfect man to represent the sacrifice for all mankind. Had Christ sinned even once, He would have received the punishment on the cross for His own sin. Had there been even one sin in the life of Jesus Christ, He could not have died in place of all mankind. He would have died for His own sin. Therefore He had to be perfect.

And He was. The Bible says that since He had made himself a man, he was tempted as all men are, but He never sinned. He remained perfect. So when God unleashed His punishment on Christ at Calvary, Christ was worthy to receive the punishment for all the sins of the world. No other man would have been worthy, because every other man deserves punishment for his own sin. Jesus was the only perfect One, and only He could meet the standard for keeping the covenant with God.

The old covenant or Old Testament was based on obedience. If man could obey God, then God would bless man. The problem was that no man would ever be able to remain perfect, without sin. Adam couldn't do it. Noah couldn't do it. Abram couldn't do it. Moses couldn't do it. King David couldn't do it. No matter how hard any of us have tried, we have all sinned. The Bible says that *all* have fallen short of the glory of God. There is no man who has been, or would be, perfect enough to keep this covenant, except Christ Himself.

God knows this. He knew that Abram would never be able to fulfill the covenant. God's part of the covenant was to release all of His love and not withhold Himself from Abram in any way. But to fulfill Abram's part of the covenant, Abram would have to love God with all of his heart, soul, mind, and body without ever putting anything or anyone else before God. Perfection was the requirement for this covenant.

Many people think that they are loving God with all of their heart and soul, when they really are not. If I loved God always and completely, I would never do anything that was offensive to Him. There is no love in sin. When I sin against God in any way, in that moment, I am not loving God. I may love Him in my heart as much as is humanly possible, but in that moment, I am not loving Him perfectly, as required by the old covenant. I am disregarding Him, taking Him for granted. So sin always involves putting something or someone in front of God. That's not love. No man, no firepot, would ever be able to keep the old covenant.

Consider this for a moment. God knew that Abram would never be able to keep his part of the covenant, so God appeared in both the form of a blazing torch *and* a smoking firepot. This was God's way of saying, "I will fulfill my part of the covenant, and I will fulfill your part of the covenant." God did not ask Abram to do something he was unable to do. Instead He took Abram's place in the form of a firepot. This was a foreshadowing of the new covenant.

During the Last Supper, Jesus lifted the cup and said, "This cup is the new covenant in my blood, which is poured out for you" (Luke 22:20). The new covenant does not require perfection. It requires faith. So many times the Scripture says "in Christ." This is because it is in Christ—in the person of Christ, the firepot from heaven—that we remain in covenant with God.

The new covenant did not make the old covenant obsolete. This is why Jesus said that He did not come to abolish the Law but to fulfill it. He fulfilled every law. This means that God, through His Son, Jesus Christ, continues to keep His part of the covenant, even when Abram fails. He continues to keep His part of the covenant, even when you and I fail. He knew we would fail just as Abram did, and all of mankind *has* failed. But in His foreknowledge of our inability to love perfectly without sin, He fulfilled our part of the covenant Himself. So now, even when we mess up, God still releases His love and His plans into our lives, as long as we maintain our faith in Jesus Christ.

Do not live in fear of not being a good enough Christian. Do not let your past sins or mistakes weigh you down. The Devil is a liar! Do not let yourself be convinced that the plans of God for you are gone because you really sinned in the worst way or made an unbelievable mistake. God has always known you would not be perfect. He has always known that you would sin and fail, but He fulfills your part of the covenant.

Remember, this is God's answer to Abram's asking, "How can I know the promise is going to come to pass?" Abram had waited and waited. God had made some big promises, but nothing had happened yet. Sometimes the promises of God take time. The promise is not the goal. The goal, for God, is to bring you where you need to be spiritually so that the promise will not corrupt your spirit by causing you to take God for granted, to become conceited, or to live as if you don't need God. That is His goal for our lives, and the promise is part of the journey to get us there.

Waiting for the promise is part of the journey. God wants to do amazing things in our lives, but first He must prepare our hearts to handle such spiritual riches. God's answer to Abram was to make a covenant with him and to fulfill both sides of the covenant. God's answer to Abram was that He would finish what He'd started. Waiting for God can be difficult, but God's promise is that we don't have to wonder if God is going to show up. We just have to learn to wait until He does show up, because He will finish His part.

You may feel like Abram, wondering when God is going to do what He said He would do. You may be waiting for protection, for deliverance, for blessing, for comfort, for vision, for supply. During this time, don't think for a minute that God has forgotten you. God was reminding Abram that He had not forgotten him. The promise was not there yet, but God still remembered it and would be faithful.

God has not forgotten your prayers, your tears, your needs, and your desires. The Devil will tell you that you are not good enough. He will remind you of your sin and tell you how unworthy you are of any blessings. He will run you down. He will make fun of you. He will bring up the words you heard from an angry mother or a drunk father. The demons from your childhood will whisper to you the words that hurt so badly and broke your spirit. The words of your ex-husband, older brother, or stepsister will ring in your ears.

Do not listen! *Do not listen!* The Devil is a liar, and God is with you! You remain always on the mind of God. Your name is always on His lips. His plans for your life are always in His hand. He will sustain you. He will hold you up. You will rise out of the ashes. God will bring you through. Praise Him now for what He is going to do.

Do not let the Devil bring up all of your mistakes and sin. Your part of the covenant has been fulfilled by Jesus Christ. You don't have to be perfect or sinless. Your mistakes are not enough to make the covenant null and void. Your sin can't destroy God's plan for your life. Your immaturity will not forfeit His plan for your life. Take heart. Be encouraged.

God is with you, and He will be faithful!

Preparing the Sacrifices

"Then birds of prey came down on the carcasses, but Abram drove them away" (Genesis 15:11 NIV).

God fulfilled His part of the covenant, and He fulfilled Abram's part of the covenant. One thing God did not do was to prepare and protect the sacrifices. God could have easily prepared these animals and set them in place. After all, He brought forth a blazing torch and a firepot out of nowhere. He could have done this with one word from His mouth. Instead, He called upon Abram to prepare the sacrifices, and then, when the birds of prey came, it was Abram who protected the sacrifices.

It is always interesting to see what God does—and what He does *not* do. God can do anything, but He does not spoil us. Instead He invites us into His work, into His mission. We get to be part of supernatural miracles through prayer. We get to be part of the salvation of others through witnessing.

Here, God did the heavy lifting (though it was not difficult for Him) by producing the blazing torch and the firepot and by putting Abram to sleep. But Abram had responsibility too. God took care of Abram's part in walking through the blood, because He knew that imperfect Abram would never be able to keep his part of the covenant. But He did call upon Abram to gather the sacrifices, prepare them, and protect them.

Sacrifices are such an interesting thing in Scripture, because we first have God calling upon the people to bring sacrifices. He then goes to great length in describing when and how the animals are to be prepared and slaughtered and what is to be done with the blood and the inner parts of the sacrifice.

Later, the Lord despises the sacrifices. Throughout the Old Testament, it is clear that God does not want sacrificial animals. He does not want the blood of sheep and goats and bulls. He has no use for the sacrifices themselves. We must look deeper to see God's intention for offerings and sacrifices.

We could say the very same about any kind of sacrifice or offering. For example, we do not take offerings in church every Sunday morning because God spends all of His money by Saturday night and needs more on Sunday mornings. God does not need your money any more now than He needed all of the offerings and sacrifices in the Old Testament. With this understanding, we have to ask, then, what was the purpose of all the sacrifices prescribed by God in the Old Testament. A person could get very confused—and I have—trying to figure out all of the different sacrifices that God desired, when He desired Him, and how He wanted the sacrifices prepared and offered.

It seems that this was going on constantly throughout the Old Testament. There are definite times in the Old Testament where the people stopped offering sacrifices, but not because that was what God wanted. The Old Testament teaches us that God did not want anyone coming into His presence empty-handed. The people were to be giving to Him always. God required and desired the ceremonies and rituals of the sacrifice, but it was never about the actual sacrifice. God wants us to give to Him now, but it is really not about the actual offering we give.

"'Has not my hand made all these things, and so they came into being?'" declares the Lord. "'This is the one I esteem: he who is humble and contrite in spirit, and trembles at my word. But whoever sacrifices a bull is like one who kills a man, and whoever offers a lamb, like one who breaks a dog's neck; whoever makes a grain offering is like one who presents pig's blood, and whoever burns memorial incense, like one who worships an idol. They have chosen their own ways, and their souls delight in their abominations'" (Isaiah 66:2–3 NIV).

During the history of Israel, God was increasingly clear that His desire was to have a relationship with His people, not the sacrifices they offered. There were many ceremonies and rituals in the Old Testament prescribed by God for His people. Even in the New Testament, God had prescribed ceremonies, rituals, and offerings.

Church is a ritual that God has prescribed, and the Bible says that we are not to give up meeting together. Worship and praise are rituals. Do you ever wonder why music is such a big part of worship? It always has been, even in the Old Testament. Songs are ceremonies. When you sing a song you have sung all of your life, you are participating in a ceremony.

Tithes and offerings are ritualistic offerings. The only compliment the Pharisees ever received from Christ was that they were tithing and giving offerings. A tithe is ten percent of a person's gross income. To give a certain amount at prescribed times and places is a ceremony, a ritual. Communion, baptism, baby dedications, and weddings are all ceremonies and rituals that God has prescribed—even during this New Testament period. God's reason for these is not in the ceremony itself but in what the ceremony symbolizes.

God is quite aware of how quickly our attention moves on. One of the children's movies that I have enjoyed watching is called *Up*. In this movie, there is a dog who has a technological device around his neck that allows people to hear and understand his thoughts in human language. The dog will be talking to other characters in the movie, when suddenly his head snaps to the side, his body tenses up, and his mechanical device blurts his single thought: "Squirrel!" Throughout the movie, when the pooch should be involved with the plot, a squirrel will distract him.

There are lots of squirrels in our lives. We are distracted and become so busy so easily. God knew that, because of our nature to be so consumed by the moment, we would forget things that are far more important but don't seem so in the moment. We have all put off calling Mom or Dad because of our busy schedules. We do not find the time to play with our kids because of the whirlwind of pressures we live in every day. Our nature is to do the very same thing to God. So He instituted ceremonies, rituals, and sacrifices.

The Passover was the biggest ritual and offering for the Israelites in Bible times. God commanded that the Passover be kept forever. That's how important it was to Him. Ceremonies are ordained by God, because they force us, under His command, to step off the merry-go-round of life and remember. Communion forces us to remember God's sacrifice for our sins. Church, especially worship, causes us to stop and give thanks to the Lord for all He has done. Giving our tithes reminds us that we are dependent upon God's favor to supply our needs, not a particular job or person. The purpose of God's blood covenant with Abram was to give him an experience that he would never forget. He never wanted Abram to forget that He would fulfill His promise.

If you have gotten out of the habit of participating in the ceremonies of church, communion, praise, worship, daily bread (the Word of God), baptism, and tithing, go back to them. Don't just go through the motions of the ceremony; embrace the meaning. Do not eat of the bread or drink of the wine without taking a few moments to remember the broken body of Christ and His blood, spilt so that you might be reconciled to God. Do not go to church and sit there like a bump on a log, but embrace the purpose of worship, praise, fellowship, and the Word of God. All of these ceremonies are designed to stop your brain from spinning long enough to remember and treasure the God who loves you and who has great plans for Your life.

Without the sacrifices, there is no covenant. Setting up the sacrifice is the task God has given to us. He knew we would not be able to walk through the blood and remain perfect, but He does ask us to maintain the sacrifices to help us stop and remember that He has been good to us and will keep His promises. He wants our hearts, our minds, our love, our affection, and our loyalty. He wants us—not our songs, our sermons, or our money but us.

He is jealous for us, because He knows that any other lover (god) will take us down a path of destruction. His love for us—though at times it can seem pushy—is to keep us from those things that can cause great harm in our lives. He wants our hearts and souls, not our sacrifices. But it is our sacrifices that cause us to pause and take time for this relationship with Him. His most wonderful plans for our lives will not be found, unless we continually prepare the sacrifices of God.

The Prosperity of God

God took Abram through a blood covenant, but He put Abram to sleep, and He Himself covered both sides of the covenant. God will take care of His part of the covenant by being everything to us. But He also took care of our part of the covenant—the requirement to be perfect—by sending His only begotten Son, Jesus Christ, to live a sinless life. Abram simply prepared the sacrifice and protected it from the birds of prey. But keep this in mind: it was God who gave Abram the wealth to prepare these sacrifices. God prospered Abram, and Abram was able to prepare the sacrifices. God wants to prosper you as well.

If we want to remain in God's covenant and His plans for our lives, we must prepare the sacrifices. We must give. It is not a matter of whether or not we *want* to give; we *must* give. When we stop giving, we remove ourselves, little by little, from God's plan for our lives. This wonderful plan that He has for us will not come to pass if we do not do our part. We are to give all of ourselves—not part and not some. All of our time and talent belongs to God. All of our money belongs to God. God is then gracious. He does not ask everyone to spend his life in full-time ministry. He does not expect us to spend every moment of our lives in church. He also wants us to have fun and enjoy life. We give to Him, and He gives back to us.

God does not expect every penny we make to go back to the poor or to the church. He wants us to enjoy the blessings that come from the wealth He gives to us, no matter what level of wealth it is. In fact, His covenant with Abram was that He would make Abram's name great and make him into a great nation. This can't happen without wealth.

This is what we are taught about wealth. "But remember the Lord your God, for it is he who gives you the ability to produce wealth, and so confirms his covenant, which he swore to your forefathers, as it is today" (Deuteronomy 8:18 NIV).

God's plan is for your life to be blessed, very blessed. It is to be so blessed that it overflows onto your children and grandchildren for a thousand generations (Exodus 20:6). The Bible says that a wise man leaves an inheritance for his children's children. In other words, there is enough wealth to last for generations.

Don't misunderstand what I am saying! Money is not the blessing. Wealth is the means by which God blesses. It is not the *only* means, but it is one way that God blesses. The purpose of the blessings is to display His love for His children and to distinguish His children from the rest of the world so that the world might take notice and begin to follow the same God to whom we give glory for any and all blessings we have.

Ecclesiastes says that money is the answer for everything (Ecclesiastes 10:19). This simply means that if you want a roof over your head, it takes money. If you want to feed and clothe your family, it takes money. If you want to send Bibles to Africa, it takes money. If you want to have a building to gather and worship, it takes money. God has given us the ability to produce wealth in order to confirm His covenant to us. Out of what He has given to us, we must give back. We must prepare the sacrifice.

Too many of us have fallen into the mind-set that God wants us to endure poverty and "go without" all of our lives. There are certainly times when the Lord will call someone to this kind of life. God may put us in places where we have to live in poverty in order for us to come into contact with those we would never contact except through poverty. But God's plan of world redemption is to reveal His goodness through the blessings of His people. He wants you to be blessed.

However, if He blesses us before we are ready, we have a tendency to fall in love with the blessing more than the blesser, and this will kill us. Therefore, He gives to us as He matures us, so that when the blessing falls into our laps, we are not corrupted. God's desire to bless us never goes away. We must never assume that our lives, as they are right now, are as good as they get. This goes against the Word.

"The path of the righteous is like the first gleam of dawn, shining ever brighter till the full light of day" (Proverbs 4:18 NIV). This is God's plan for those who follow Him earnestly. When He comes into our lives, it is like the dawn. Isaiah taught that for those who had been living in the shadow of death, a light had dawned. But God's plan for our lives is that our days will become better and better throughout life, comparing that progression to the rising of the sun at dawn to the full light of day.

This does not mean that you will have fewer and fewer problems and issues, but it does mean that God intends for His prosperity in us to be ever-increasing. It is a prosperity of the heart, the mind, the soul, and the body. The problems don't go away, but this Scripture means that God will give us ever-increasing strength to overcome, ever-increasing power for miracles, and ever-increasing wisdom in decisions. With every trial, we will come out more anointed than before as children of God.

This is God's plan for you, and it is God's plan for world redemption. As His people mature to where they can handle this wealth of blessing without becoming idolatrous, those who are lost and blind will see the difference in their lives. God intends for the people of God to be so blessed that those without God take note. When we love those who have little and we give our testimonies, they will hear the reason that we have great blessings in our lives: "It's all because of Jesus!"

God wants to bless you, not only because He loves you, but because He loves every person you will ever come in contact with. He intends for the blessings in your life to be a beacon of light to draw others to you and, in the process, to Him. So stop settling for less than what God wants for you.

It's not just about money. When we read about God's plan for our lives, Scripture says that God wants us to prosper. We often minimize the meaning behind this word. Too often we try to equate prosperity with money or financial blessing. But God gives money to both the righteous and the unrighteous. Having money does not mean that we have the favor of God.

The love of money also has the potential to produce wealth, but wealth produced through the worship of money will never be a blessing. A person can have tons of money. *You* might have tons of money. This does not mean that God is pleased with you. However, God does bless with money. Money can be a curse, and it can be a blessing. It is not evidence of blessing from God. It could be, but it may not be.

Consider these Scriptures. "To the man who pleases him, God gives wisdom, knowledge and happiness, but to the sinner he gives the task of gathering and storing up wealth to hand it over to the one who pleases God" (Ecclesiastes 2:26 NIV). "The blessing of the Lord brings wealth, and he adds no trouble to it" (Proverbs 10:22 NIV).

Those who are not trusting in God struggle with money. They struggle with not having enough. They struggle with protecting what they have. They worry about how to make more, get more, have more money. In this way, God uses the worry to turn people back to Him. At the same time, He blesses those who trust Him by supplying all of their needs when He takes from one and gives to another.

But to those who live to please God, the blessing of money comes without the heartache. It comes without the stress and the worry. When the Lord brings wealth, He adds no trouble to it. I love that. The prosperity of God is all-inclusive. He does not prosper us financially without also prospering us in patience, wisdom, joy, and peace. The peace and joy in our souls is more indicative of the prosperity of God in our lives.

There seem to be two differing thoughts on this subject. One thought says that if God is pleased with us, we will become wealthy. I don't agree with that. The other thought is that if God is pleased with us, we will live in poverty. I don't agree with that, either. God's plan for our lives is to prosper us in every way. Each path of prosperity in our lives will only enhance the other avenues of prosperity. When God gives us the prosperity of peace, it will not cause us to be content to live without blessings. It will allow us to endure times of hardship without giving us a sense that life is as good as it is ever going to get.

When God gives us prosperity in the form of wealth, it will not cause us to be up to our eyeballs in stress. This wealth will enhance our sense of peace, not destroy it. This peace will alleviate the fear of failing. The peace of God will make every decision about our wealth less threatening, because we know that God will continue to provide for us, even if we make a mistake. We will be confident that He will give us the wealth of success as much as He gives us the wealth of humility. He will give us the wealth of answered prayer as much as the wealth of patience, as we learn to wait when He does not answer. One prosperity does not negate another.

Give your life to God, seeking Him every day and believing that He will bless you.

The Power of Giving Back

The Lord called Abram into a covenant. He sent Abram to gather and prepare the sacrifices. God reminded Abram of His promise to fulfill an incredible plan for Abram's life. When Abram asked God, "How can I know for sure?" God led him into a blood covenant. But God Himself took Abram's place by walking through the covenant ceremony using the symbolism of a firepot, even as He represented Himself as a blazing torch. It was God's way of promising Abram that He would work out His plan for Abram's life, and that Abram's part of the process was to gather and prepare the sacrifices.

The Lord desires a covenant with you. This covenant includes a plan to prosper you, not to harm you, and to give you a future (Jeremiah 29:11). God sent His Son, Jesus Christ, to walk through the blood for you so that your own sin and mistakes do not mess everything up. But you have a part. You are to gather the sacrifices and prepare them.

When we enter into a covenant with God, it means that we are not at the mercy of the world. The world is not the proprietor of our lives. We are citizens of heaven, and our God has promised to protect us, to bless us, and to give us a life that is ever-increasing in blessing—like the dawning sun to noonday. Too many Christians feel that we are helpless victims of everything that is going on in the world. But we are not.

"So shall they fear the name of the Lord from the west, and his glory from the rising of the sun. When the enemy shall come in like a flood, the Spirit of the Lord shall lift up a standard against him" (Isaiah 59:19 NIV).

While you are on this journey with God, you can be assured of a few things. You can be assured that there will be trials and tribulations. Jesus promised this. You will face hard times, because the earth has been cursed, and there is sickness and disease. You will face hard times, because God loves the human race so much that He has given everyone the freedom of choice, and many people choose badly. These people will hurt you, betray you, attack you, and generally make life difficult for you. Because mankind is sinful, even the people in your life that truly love God will still sin at times and hurt you. You can be assured of a lot of pain in this life.

You can also be assured that every time the Enemy tries to use these events to crush your spirit and break your heart, God will intervene. But our covenant with God goes further than this. If we uphold our side of the covenant, God's promises will help us to avoid much of the pain in this world and enjoy more blessing from God.

Let me give you an example. The Bible says to have nothing to do with an angry man (Proverbs 22:24). How many women could have avoided abuse if they had followed this advice? How much more blessed would their children have been if they had not been exposed to the angry men in their mother's life. This is the covenant. Following the covenant saves us from so much pain.

We are currently in a horrible place in our nation. When it comes to moral issues, our entire culture seems to be moving toward positions that are displeasing to God. I don't care if you are a Republican, Democrat, or Independent. If you are a Christian and believe the Bible to be the Word of God, then you know that God hates abortion. He *hates* abortion!

Our nation has moved toward abortion for one reason. It is not because of the unbelievers in our nation. It is not because of corrupt politicians. It is not because of Clinton, Bush, Obama, or any other president. Our nation is moving away from God, because Christians have not kept the covenant. We have been called to evangelize. That is, we have been commanded by God, as part of this covenant, to go out and tell people about God and the gospel of Jesus Christ.

But in our nation, we have not done this. We have bowed down to politically correct standards, and we have cowered behind our own fear of mentioning the name of Jesus Christ to anyone. As a result of not keeping the covenant, the influence of the church of Jesus Christ has fallen to an all-time low in our nation. If the church is not spreading its influence, you can be sure that the god of this world (2 Corinthians 4:4) is spreading his influence.

Our nation is falling away from God. The power to turn our nation around has always been with us. We blame the downfall of our nation on the amoral society around us, but God lays the fault for our nation's separation from godly principles at the feet of believers. Even now, as believers, we have the power to transform our nation and move it toward the Lord. But the answer will not come through politics or protesting abortion clinics. It will not come by arguing theology on Facebook. All of these are needed at the right time, but the real power is found in seeking after the Lord to change the heart of our nation.

Here is a very powerful Scripture: "If my people, who are called by my name, will humble themselves and pray and seek my face and turn from their wicked ways, then will I hear from heaven and will forgive their sin and will heal their land" (2 Chronicles 7:14 NIV).

The covenant into which we have entered with God says that if those of us who believe will turn back to God, He will heal our land. Right now, the church of Jesus Christ in the United States of America has the power to turn our nation around. It's part of the covenant. If we—not unbelievers, not corrupt politicians, not presidents, but *we*—will turn back to God, He will then release His part of the covenant. He will influence the hearts of unbelievers and politicians to create and uphold policies that reflect the values of Christians.

I am not trying to get all political on you or anything. I am just trying to choose one area that is right before our eyes to reveal how much power there is in this covenant. There is nothing in this world that can overtake you or overcome you if you are upholding your part of the covenant. In every situation, God will release power for you to overcome and overtake what the world is trying to do to you. Also, when you uphold your part of the covenant, God will destroy many of the plans of the Enemy so that you never even experience some attacks. You have been given power through covenant-living to ensure that your family is blessed, your church is blessed, and your nation is blessed. They will all be attacked, but they will all be blessed, and they will all overcome.

You are not powerless in this world. On the contrary, by upholding your part of the covenant, you release the power of God all around you, and there is no layoff, recession, depression, sickness, death, divorce, abuse, or molestation that can stand against our God. We must learn to uphold our part of the covenant—to gather, prepare, and protect the sacrifices.

Abram took the sacrifices, slaughtered them, and created the required path. He took what God had blessed him with and gave it back to God. If we are going to see the plans of God manifest in our lives, we must learn to give back to God what He has given to us. This is imperative. Even the Devil understands this, and that is why the spirit of this world does not pressure people to save money, spend it wisely, or give it away to help others. The spirit of this world, the spirit of Satan, pressures people to spend more than what they can afford and to take advantage of credit until they are paying more on interest than on principle. It pushes people into living from paycheck to paycheck in order to empty the hands of people so that they have nothing to give back to God.

This is not just a financial issue. The Bible says that Satan is out to steal, kill, and destroy (John 10:10). He is trying to deplete us of any blessings God has given to us—not just to make us miserable but also to keep us from having anything to give back. He tries to steal our joy so that we won't praise. He tries to steal our assurance so that we don't worship. He tries to steal our time so we won't serve. He tries to steal our health so we can't live each day to the fullest. He does not want us to give, but the plans of God will never come to pass in our lives until we learn the principle of giving.

God works through kingdom principles, and this is something lost in a country that is a democracy. Even the current kingdoms of our society are nothing what they were like in Bible times. Let's walk through a meeting between King Solomon and the queen of Sheba to expound on God's kingdom principles in the area of giving.

When the queen of Sheba heard about the fame of Solomon and his relation to the name of the Lord, she came to test him with hard questions. Arriving at Jerusalem with a very great caravan—with camels carrying spices, large quantities of gold, and precious stones—she came to Solomon and talked with him about all that she had on her mind. Solomon answered all her questions; nothing was too hard for the king to explain to her.

When the queen of Sheba saw all the wisdom of Solomon and the palace he had built, the food on his table, the seating of his officials, the attending servants in their robes, his cupbearers, and the burnt offerings he made at the temple of the Lord, she was overwhelmed.

She said to the king, "The report I heard in my own country about your achievements and your wisdom is true. But I did not believe these things until I came and saw with my own eyes. Indeed, not even half was told me; in wisdom and wealth you have far exceeded the report I heard. How happy your men must be! How happy your officials, who continually stand before you and hear your wisdom! Praise be to the Lord your God, who has delighted in you and placed you on the throne of Israel. Because of the Lord's eternal love for Israel, he has made you king, to maintain justice and righteousness."

And she gave the king 120 talents of gold, large quantities of spices, and precious stones. Never again were so many spices brought in as those the queen of Sheba gave to King Solomon.

(Hiram's ships brought gold from Ophir; and from there they brought great cargoes of almugwood and precious stones. The king used the almugwood to make supports for the temple of the Lord and for the royal palace, and to make harps and lyres for the musicians. So much almugwood has never been imported or seen since that day.)

King Solomon gave the queen of Sheba all she desired and asked for, besides what he had given her out of his royal bounty. Then she left and returned with her retinue to her own country. (1 Kings 10:1–13 NIV)

In this passage are some kingdom principles that are key to our understanding the idea of giving back to God what He has given to us. The queen of Sheba had heard of Solomon and his wisdom and wealth. During this period, if two opposing kings—or in this case, a queen—wanted to see who was greater, each would give gifts to the other.

Scripture says that when the queen of Sheba brought in all her gifts, never had so much been brought into the kingdom. This was not just a simple gesture. This was the queen's way of saying, "I have so much wealth that I can easily part with all of this. I am so great that I can give all of this away." She was challenging Solomon, displaying her greatness to see if Solomon was as great as she was. It was a monumental challenge.

In verse 13, the match ended when King Solomon gave the queen of Sheba all she desired and asked for. But it went beyond that. Their meeting was also recorded in 2 Chronicles. "King Solomon gave the queen of Sheba all she desired and asked for; he gave her more than she had brought to him" (2 Chronicles 9:12 NIV). It was the custom that one king giving gifts to another was a challenge for the recipient to give back even more than he had received. Solomon displayed his greatness by giving to the queen what she had given to him—and more.

And so it is with God. When we give to Him, He will always display His greatness by giving back to us more than we gave to Him. This is a kingdom principle. God is so much greater than we are that He will always out-give us when we give to Him. It provides Him with an opportunity to show His greatness in our lives. He does this because He loves us and wants to bless us. He also does this because He wants His greatness to shine out of our lives for others to see—with the hope that they will see His greatness and turn to Him.

The blessings you have received from God are nothing compared to what He wants to give you in your life. However, to move forward on this journey with God, your part of the covenant is to take the blessings He has given you and give them back to Him. Then He will give you even more.

Satan has produced a tsunami of pressure in the spirit of this world to strip us of everything we have—so that we can never give back our sacrifices to the Lord. We must diligently protect our ability to give back to the Lord. We must give back to Him out of what He has given to us. If you have any joy, give a sacrifice of praise. If you have any healing, give Him a sacrifice of song. If you have received any victory, shout to the Lord! If you have received any provision, give back to Him your tithes and offerings. He will always give back to you more than you could ever give to Him.

Life is the greatest blessing we've been given. As our part of the covenant, we must give it back to Him. We must lay our life before Him and ask, "Lord, what would you have me do with my life?" This is a kingdom principle.

"If you have any encouragement from being united with Christ, if any comfort from his love, if any fellowship with the Spirit, if any tenderness and compassion, then make my joy complete by being like-minded, having the same love, being one in spirit and purpose. Do nothing out of selfish ambition or vain conceit, but in humility consider others better than yourselves. Each of you should look not only to your own interests, but also to the interests of others" (Philippians 2:1–4 NIV).

This Scripture says it all. It is God's plan for you to take all that He has given you and use it for others, for ministry. Perhaps you are expecting me to say that everyone should be a pastor of a church or a missionary or something like that. Well, that could be the case for you. It could be that God wants you to go to seminary. But before you close this book or turn off your Kindle, let me say that God needs people everywhere.

Let's face it: there are people you work with who would never grace the doors of a church. That is the last place they would ever go. They would never turn on the television and watch any preacher. But every day, they are getting paid by someone to come and sit right next to you. If you are willing, God will provide an opportunity to talk about how good He has been to you. Little by little, these talks—in the context of the character, integrity, and love by which you live your life—will have influence. One day, these coworkers *will* go to church, but not because of a full-time preacher, evangelist, or missionary. It will be because of the secret agent that God planted right next to them. Are we not all missionaries and preachers wherever God has planted us?

One of my favorite ministries that our church takes part in every year is called Angel Tree. This is a ministry where local churches "adopt" children whose parents, one or both, are in prison. We take these children gifts and love. We convey the message that God loves them. I love this ministry, because it is a small part of God's plan to reverse the generational curse that might be on these children.

This ministry was started by Chuck Colson, who was the biggest fall guy in the Watergate scandal during the Nixon presidency, and he went to prison. Maybe he had to go to prison to find Christ. Maybe he already knew Christ. Either way, God used Colson's sin and mistakes during Watergate to plant an agent in a place that definitely needed God. Out of his experience, Colson started Prison Fellowship Ministries and Angel Tree. He did not pastor a church. He was not a missionary in Africa. He was planted in a prison to find God and to share Christ. He found God's plan for his life—in prison.

God has given you life. Now, prepare your sacrifices and give your life back to Him. Wherever He puts you, whether at home with your children, in a factory with thousands of coworkers, or on a recreational softball team, give your life to Him. Let God use your life for His glory. Give to Him, and He will give back to you. "Give, and it will be given to you. A good measure, pressed down, shaken together and running over, will be poured into your lap. For with the measure you use, it will be measured to you" (Luke 6:38 NIV).

God's plans for our lives will never come to pass until we learn to give our sacrifices to the Lord, who has given us everything that is good and right in our lives. I cannot sit here and tell you who God wants you to marry. I cannot tell you what profession God wants for you. I can't tell you which outfit God wants you to wear today. I can't tell you any of that. For the most part, God doesn't tell us these things audibly. But He will put something in your heart, or He will open a door that will place you into a certain family, job, or church. His plans for your life are dependent upon these things.

God can release His dreams for our lives anywhere we might be—even in prison. The key is for us to prepare the sacrifices. We must learn to give back to Him every blessing He has given us, from our money to our minds. Giving our blessings back to Him by giving to others will release His plans for us, regardless of our geographic location or professional career.

The journey that you are on is God's instrument to lead you to this surrender. He is not leading you toward a certain education, but He will provide opportunities and open doors for you to get that education. The education is not God's plan for your life. The education will merely place you in situations where you can give back to Him—if you have allowed God to prepare your heart for surrender.

The beautiful baby you just had is not the totality of God's plan for you. The baby will bring you to a place of joy and tears, happiness and sadness, worry and stress. God will use all of these to prepare your heart for sacrifice so that you might give back to Him all of the blessings in your life.

And then ... then He will release His greater plan for your life. This is a plan that will fight through all of the pain and struggle and get better and better with time. Wherever you are in life is God's instrument, at this moment, to bring about your surrender to give back to Him. Get ready, because He will pour a wonderful life into you—pressed down, shaken together, and running over. Praise the Lord!

Protecting the Sacrifices

"Then birds of prey came down on the carcasses, but Abram drove them away" (Genesis 15:11 NIV).

At some point on our journey with God, we must understand the nature of the journey. We are not taking a leisurely stroll down a beautiful path with daisies on either side shining brightly in the sun. No, we are at war. We are at war for our own souls. We are at war for those under us spiritually. We are at war for our families and friends.

I have never seen the horrors of physical war. My church is full of men and women who have been deployed and have seen the most horrific things. They have seen body parts blown clean off the body, and they have walked among the dead. While deployed, they faced enormous pressure, knowing that they could be attacked at any moment. Enemy combatants were not stupid. There was a clear understanding on their part that they could not overcome the training, numbers, and equipment of our own forces. So they did not fight face-to-face or in the open. They disguised themselves. They strapped bombs to the bodies of pregnant women and children and sent them into heavily populated areas.

Our Enemy, the Devil, is the architect of this style of warfare. The apostle Paul warned the New Testament churches to guard themselves against the enemy outside the walls of the church, but to also guard themselves against the wolves in sheep's clothing—those in the church whose motives and goals were not pure. These internal attacks catch us off guard. They surprise us and deflate us. Our friends and family come after us unexpectedly, like a pregnant woman strapped to a makeshift bomb.

Before I went into the ministry, I was a football coach and Spanish teacher at a local high school in Waco, Texas. We moved there so my wife could attend Baylor University on scholarships. We got involved in the church there, and God began to renew a call to preach that He had once placed on my heart during high school. It was a very strange time, and my wife and I walked through it with excitement and peace. We thought to ourselves that we were giving our lives fully to God in ministry and it was going to be awesome. I don't think we would have admitted it, and we knew it was not true, but we had an expectation that as people given totally to the purposes of God, we would be fully protected. But the attacks came quickly.

We had befriended a couple in the church. They were a little bit older and, in our eyes, they were a little bit wiser. They had already been through much of what life could throw at a person, and they were still married and still loved the Lord. We became close to them.

When the pastor and church board began to consider me for the position of youth pastor, our friends approached the senior pastor and began to fight against the idea of me becoming the youth pastor. They fought hard against us without ever saying a word to us. The people we had trusted and leaned on were walking into our lives with hidden bombs. We had really believed that this couple, more than anyone else, would celebrate what God was doing in our lives. We were wrong. We were at war with the Enemy.

Too many of us do not live life, spiritually, as if we are at war. We see destruction from the attacks of the Enemy and chalk it up to coincidence. We see bad things happen and figure that they were inevitable. I want to take a second and remind you that God is a God of war and a God of miracles. When God fights, He has His own bombs. He changes hearts. He heals brokenness. He directs someone to send a check in the mail. He allows someone's sin to completely remove them from your life and your situation. We don't have to sit back and just accept the high points and low points in life as circumstance. God is in control, and we have His ear.

"May the Lord answer you when you are in distress; may the name of the God of Jacob protect you. May he send you help from the sanctuary and grant you support from Zion. May he remember all your sacrifices and accept your burnt offerings. Selah. May he give you the desire of your heart and make all your plans succeed. We will shout for joy when you are victorious and will lift up our banners in the name of our God. May the Lord grant all your requests. Now I know that the Lord saves his anointed; he answers him from his holy heaven with the saving power of his right hand. Some trust in chariots and some in horses, but we trust in the name of the Lord our God" (Psalm 20:1–7 NIV).

Scripture says that the heart of the king is in the hands of God, and He can move it any direction He chooses, just as He moves the water on the earth (Proverbs 21:1). It is not only the believer who is submitted to God who can be moved by God. God moves the heart of whomever He chooses. He can change the heart of a believer or an unbeliever. He can move the heart of the kindest person or the vilest. Our lives are not dependent upon rulers and authorities in the heavenly realm, nor do they depend on the people we come in contact with each day. Our lives are in the hands of God, and He moves mountains for those who call upon His name!

We are at war! People will attack. Even those who have been your closest friends will turn on you at times. The temptations that people will put before you and the temptations of your own mind are attacks from the Devil. But God's plans for our lives cannot be stopped by any person or any devil. "For our struggle is not against flesh and blood, but against the rulers, against the authorities, against the powers of this dark world and against the spiritual forces of evil in the heavenly realms" (Ephesians 6:12).

Someone may be saying, "Well, what about my ex? She keeps on trying to …" "What about my boss? He is such a jerk!" "What about my husband? He is so controlling and demanding."

Stop it! Stop it! Stop giving them more power than they have. Either God is the God He claims to be, the One who has all authority in heaven and earth, or He is nothing but a liar. You must decide today what you believe. This war will never be won—and you will never enjoy the fantastic plans that God has for you—unless you believe that God is on your side and that He is able to defeat the Enemy at every turn.

Consider this Scripture and pay special attention to the word *must*. "And without faith it is impossible to please God, because anyone who comes to him *must* believe that he exists and that he rewards those who earnestly seek him" (Hebrews 11:6 NIV).

Neither you nor I can come to God unless we believe He exists *and* that He rewards those who earnestly seek him. We must believe that God wants to do good things in our lives. We must believe that despite all our sin and mistakes and all that we are, God still loves us and has plans for us. Either He is God or He isn't.

Right now, you must decide. Do not try to stand on your mama's faith or your grandmother's religion. It's between you and God, and you must believe that part of God's perfect plan for you is for good things to happen. If you believe that, then you'd better also know that you are at war. God wants a covenant with you for great things to come. But you are at war for your soul, and the Devil is out to steal, kill, and destroy. Therefore, you must drive away the birds of prey.

"The thief comes only to steal and kill and destroy; I have come that they may have life, and have it to the full" (John 10:10 NIV). The Enemy is attempting to steal from you anything that you can give back to God. He is trying to keep you so busy that you no longer have time (or so you think) to read the Bible, to pray, or to go to church. He may try to steal your time with problems and issues. He may try to steal your time with promotions, success, and greater responsibilities, but rest assured, He is trying to steal your time.

The children God has blessed you with are dedicated to the Lord. We lay them in the hands of God by teaching them, praying for them, and fighting for their future and their peace. But the Enemy is out to destroy them. He knows that if He can destroy your children, He will break your heart. He will crush you.

The marriage God has given you as a blessing is under attack. The Enemy does not want you to give your marriage back to God. He understands that what is dedicated to the Lord will be blessed by the Lord. So there will be temptations. Temptresses will appear, looking for a shoulder to cry on. They will feign loyalty and respect when the lines of communication at home are struggling. They will appear to be friends and possible lovers, but they are soldiers in a war to destroy every blessing that could be given back to God. You are at war. Be vigilant! Be alert! These soldiers have hidden bombs strapped to them.

Remember that God called Abram to a wonderful covenant. God also knew that Abram could not fulfill his part of the covenant, so He put Abram to sleep and then appeared as both the blazing torch of God and the firepot of man. He fulfilled our part of the covenant so that our own weaknesses and frailties would be unable to forfeit the plans of God in our lives. But we still have responsibilities in the covenant. Our part is to prepare the sacrifices and protect them from the birds of prey.

The birds of prey will come from within and from without. People will provoke you and tempt you. Your own evil desires of the flesh will provoke you and tempt you. These are the birds of prey that are trying to ravage your offerings and sacrifices to the Lord. If you do not keep the birds of prey away, how can you give back to God?

How can you live in this covenant? You can't. None of us can. God has done the miraculous, but we have a part. We must never stop giving to the Lord, and anything that attempts to keep us from giving back to God is a bird of prey. Therefore, protect your time with God as if it is the only weapon you have against the schemes of the Enemy.

Protect your children. Teach them. Pray for them. Discipline them. Do not allow them to stray into the Enemy's camp. Dedicate them to the Lord that they might be blessed.

Protect your own spirit. Seek the Lord each day, as if He was your only salvation, because He is. Protect your dreams. Protect your aspirations. Never give up the desires of your heart, because God wants to do great things in your life, and He is able. He *is* able. Nothing can stop the plans God has for you, as long as you keep preparing the sacrifices.

Keep giving yourself to Him. Keep seeking after Him. These are your sacrifices. Protect them. Do not let anything keep you or your family out of church. If your husband won't go, love him, but do not let him keep you from worshipping the Lord everywhere you go.

Do not let anything steal your hope. The troubles of this life are the prerequisites for God's miracles. Stand up! Fight for everything dear to you. Give it all back to God. This will keep you in God's plan for your life. And He will give back to you—pressed down, shaken together, and running over. Drive the birds of prey away. Drive them far away!

"Now to him who is able to do immeasurably more than all we ask or imagine, according to his power that is at work within us, to him be glory in the church and in Christ Jesus throughout all generations, for ever and ever! Amen" (Ephesians 3:20–21 NIV).

The Firepot

It is our duty to prepare and protect the sacrifices in order to remain in God's plan for our lives. We need to fight both the spiritual battles and our own nature. We must exercise discipline to do everything necessary to prepare and protect the sacrifices, to keep the covenant active in our lives. This will bring about God's wonderful plan for us. Without this discipline, the stress and fast pace of life will drain our time and energy. We will be too tired to read Scripture each day. We will be too busy for church. We will be too distracted for prayer. We will stop giving our tithes and offerings to the church. We will leave the sacrifices unprotected, and the birds of prey will come upon them and steal them away, nullifying our covenant with God.

This new covenant negates our need to be perfect before God. Christ became the perfect sacrifice and fulfillment of the old covenant so that we might live by faith in Him. But if we walk around thinking to ourselves that Jesus died for us and now every blessing from heaven is going to fall into our laps, we are going to be sadly disappointed. Too many churches are teaching this now.

We still have responsibility in this new covenant. It is not our responsibility to erase our past sins and never sin again. This was the requirement of the Old Testament, and no one was able to do it. Instead, our responsibility is to prepare our gifts to God and to protect them from the birds of prey so that we are always able to worship and devote ourselves to God. This keeps us in the covenant. If we do not do this, we will spend eternity in heaven, but we will not have experienced all that God wanted for us here on earth.

When I consider the phrase "birds of prey," my mind goes to the 1963 Hitchcock movie called *The Birds*. These ravenous birds were horrifying in behavior and evil in appearance. But spiritual birds of prey are not always easily identifiable. Anything that distracts us from protecting our sacrifices becomes a bird of prey.

"Large crowds were traveling with Jesus, and turning to them he said: 'If anyone comes to me and does not hate his father and mother, his wife and children, his brothers and sisters—yes, even his own life—he cannot be my disciple'" (Luke 14:25–26 NIV).

Here, Christ was not teaching us that we are to hate our mothers and fathers. He was saying something outrageous to gain attention and then make a point. The point Christ was driving home was that nothing can be more important to us than God. More than that, Jesus was teaching that there are many good things—very good things, and even blessings from God—that can become birds of prey.

If I spend all of my time with my child but never spend any time with the Lord, the spiritual lessons I am able to learn and pass on to my child are very limited. Some would look at the great amount of time I spent with my son and consider me a great father, but if I never taught him wisdom to overcome the issues of this life, how good a father could I be? If I am not spending the time I need with my Lord, how will I receive the wisdom I need to pass down to my son?

So many people struggle with the idea that Abraham was later commanded by God to sacrifice his own son. God never intended to allow Abraham to go through with it, but the lesson was that not even the promises of God can become more important than God himself. Birds of prey can come in all forms—evil and innocent, sweet and nasty, demonic and angelic—and we must discipline ourselves to continually prepare and protect the sacrifices.

If God is fulfilling both His part and our part in the covenant, why must we continue to prepare and protect the sacrifices? Too often, we do not understand the importance of spiritual disciplines such as these. Such disciplines are thought to be for preachers, priests, bishops, and reverends but not for regular Mr. Joe Christian. If we miss these disciplines, we will never see the plans of God fulfilled in our lives. Wow! That is important enough to repeat. *If we miss the spiritual disciplines (preparing and protecting the sacrifices), we will never see the plans of God fulfilled in our lives.*

It doesn't matter if God's plan for you is to be a fireman, a businesswoman, a stay-at-home mom, or a custodian in a homeless shelter. God's plans for your life will never be seen without these disciplines. His plan is completely tied to your becoming the firepot that God created to go through the blood of the sacrifices.

Wait a minute, preacher man! I just read an entire chapter about how God fulfills both parts of the covenant, and now you are telling me that I am supposed to become the firepot! Well, which is it?

It's both. When we first come to God and make a covenant with Him, we are truly unable to fulfill that covenant. We do not have the perfection necessary to fulfill our part, so we will fail. But the firepot represents Christ, who became the firepot for all mankind, and He does have the perfection to fulfill all of the requirements of the covenant. All who believe in Him have fulfilled the covenant through Him. Christ was all-God and all-man at the same time. He lived not by supernatural power but the power of the Holy Spirit, the fire of God. We are called to imitate Christ by living with the same fire of God inside of us. We must be the firepot. With Christ as the "firepot man" that we could never be, we are safe in our covenant with God.

But we are not called to rest in that assurance. We are called to walk in His footprints. Our faith in Christ assures us of heaven, but God wants to bless us abundantly here on earth also. God sent His Son to be the firepot we could never be, but He credits us with the perfection of Christ. The Bible says that God credited Abraham with righteousness (perfection) because he believed God. Our faith in Christ allows us to be credited with perfection. But what is credit?

In the United States, we have abused the idea of credit. Too many people see the credit card in their wallet as free money, but the intent is that someone is allowing you to have something *now* because you will have the money for it *later*. When the Scripture says that God credits us with righteousness, it is not a free pass for sin. He has given to you all the benefits of righteousness from the moment you believe, but there is an expectation that, although you have no righteousness at that point, you will have righteousness later. We use two different terms to explain this: *imparted* and *imputed*.

Imparted righteousness is what we receive on credit because of our faith. And then God gives us commands such as this: "As obedient children, do not conform to the evil desires you had when you lived in ignorance. But just as He who called you is holy, so be holy in all you do; for it is written: 'Be holy, because I am holy'" (1 Peter 1:14–16 NIV). This is no longer speaking of imparted righteousness where we are credited with the righteousness of God. It is speaking of a righteousness that is developed within us. This is *imputed* righteousness.

In the above Scripture, Peter was quoting from the book of Leviticus, where God repeated this command three different times. It is a call to become holy. It is not as though I will become as holy as God is, for He is too high in holiness for any of us to even come close. Rather, it is a call to continually grow in our holiness. We are to strive to become more like God in the way we think and act and speak.

Philippians teaches us that our attitude should be the same as that of Christ Jesus. We are to strive to become more like God, not only in action but in attitude. David cried out to God for a pure heart. The heart is the seat of our emotions, and David asked God to make him holy, even in his emotions, so that in every situation he would feel what God feels.

Be assured of this: you cannot make yourself holy by your own actions. It is the Holy Spirit who sanctifies us (1 Corinthians 6:11). But we have to invite the Holy Spirit into every corner of our soul and spirit, giving Him permission to circumcise our hearts and cleanse us of anything in us that is displeasing to God. I cannot do that for myself, and neither can any other man.

Only God can sanctify, and He does it through His Holy Spirit. The sword of the Spirit is the Word of God (Ephesians 6:17), and the Holy Spirit takes this sword and uses it to cut away our sinful flesh, leaving only what is pure. The spiritual disciplines—preparing and protecting the sacrifices—are the instruments by which the Holy Spirit sanctifies us, making us holy before God. Righteousness cannot be imputed into our spirit by the Holy Spirit unless we continually and consistently expose ourselves to the Holy Spirit, giving Him permission to sanctify us and cut away our sin more and more as we grow in Christ.

People ask me if they have to go to church to be saved, and my answer is, "Yes and no." You need the church to get saved, because our faith comes from hearing. How can we hear unless someone preaches, and how can someone preach unless he is sent? Who is it that sends the preacher? It is the church. Without the church, Bibles would not be dispersed. Without the church, there would not be regular meetings where the Word of God is taught and learned. The church is the voice, the hands, the feet, and the touch of God. Scripture says that the church is the body and Christ is the head.

So, no, you don't have to attend a church service, but yes, you need the church. You need people who believe in Christ who are willing to spread the gospel through word and deed. It is only through some believer—also known as the church—that you heard the gospel, understood it, and continued in it.

"How, then, can they call on the one they have not believed in? And how can they believe in the one of whom they have not heard? And how can they hear without someone preaching to them? And how can they preach unless they are sent?" (Romans 10:14–15 NIV).

We don't have to attend organized religious services to find God, but we do have to meet at least informally with believers to talk and learn about God. We can't grow spiritually without the church. The church is the body of Christ wherein the fire of God resides. We can't have the fire without being part of the body. Within the body, Scripture is taught.

Scripture infuses us with the Spirit that transforms us into the firepot. It is also how we learn to walk in holiness and become a firepot, carrying the fire of God as Christ does.

The spiritual disciplines do not accomplish this on their own. However, they keep the birds of prey away and deliver us into the presence of the Holy Spirit that we might grow in our spiritual maturity and holiness.

The more we become a firepot, the more God's plan will be at work in us. The blazing torch was the light. The firepot holds the fire that illuminates and heats. God wants our passion for Him to be so hot that it lights up the world around us. An empty, cold firepot has no use, but one full of fire can cook a meal or keep someone warm. It can light a path. It becomes useful to others. A firepot carries the fire of God—wherever it goes, to whomever it touches—and creates heat and light in their lives. The more we prepare and protect the sacrifices through our spiritual disciplines, the more the Holy Spirit will perfect us, preparing us to have influence on all we come in contact with. We light a path for others to find refuge, hope, and salvation.

The plan of God for each of us is good. It is wonderful. It is full of joy and happiness. It is full of prosperity and success. It is full of strength and overcoming power and divine love. But intertwined with these, God's plan is full of doing the work of God. It is full of ministry to others—helping the helpless, loving the unlovable, reaching out to the unwanted, and influencing and transforming others to help them to escape their past and believe for their future. This ministry involves leading people to Christ and teaching them how to walk in His ways.

As the fire of God grows inside of us, our ministry to others increases. The blessings of God and the work of God cannot be separated. They are woven together. The blessings are for the purpose of helping others in every way. If we don't learn to live a holy lifestyle, we will hoard the blessings for ourselves. This defeats the purpose of the blessings. God will remove the blessings and the plans He has for us until our maturity reminds us that His blessings are to be shared with those around us.

God's plan for you might be professional baseball. It could be to marry the man that you love. It might be to work as a maid, a cab driver, or a fry cook. It might be to do things no one else in your family has ever done. It might be to travel around the world. The possibilities are endless.

But the most joyful, incredible plans that God has for you will include being used as a firepot, carrying the flame of God wherever you go. And God is sending believers everywhere. You might find yourself in many roles, jobs, situations, and scenarios. All of these could be God's plan for your life—or none of them. God's plan for your life is first found in your heart. When the fires of God in us warm the hearts of those around us, feeding them with the Word of God, *there* is the place of God's plan for you. You will never be in the right place with God until you have become the firepot of God. So, being certain of our salvation by faith, we press on to allow the Holy Spirit to perfect us.

What is the plan of God for your life? It is the journey. It is the trek. It is the walk with God that will take you to so many different places and destinations. Each destination is an opportunity to prepare and protect the sacrifices of the covenant so that you might become the firepot, carrying all the goodness of God into every life you touch. It is on this journey where you will find your smile. Your spirit will be revived, time and again. One step after another, you will find a joy unspeakable and full of glory. Maybe it is a dirt road to the farm, a superhighway to the next promotion, or a dead end in the same job for thirty years, but it is the journey that changes us, makes us, delivers us, and renews and restores us.

Who knows where your life will lead you? God has called you to a place that He will show you. The journey there, wherever "there" is, will develop you and prepare you for the plan of God. This plan is so rewarding and wonderful that He says, "No eye has seen, no ear has heard, and no mind can conceive the plans God has for you" (1 Corinthians 2:9).

Keep the birds of prey away. Protect the sacrifices. Become a firepot of God. And the most wonderful life you could ever imagine will be yours.

"When the sun had set and darkness had fallen, a smoking firepot with a blazing torch appeared and passed between the pieces. On that day the Lord made a covenant with Abram" (Genesis 15:17–18 NIV).

For Generations

"Then God said, 'Take your son, your only son, Isaac, whom you love, and go to the region of Moriah. Sacrifice him there as a burnt offering on one of the mountains I will tell you about'" (Genesis 22:2 NIV).

This has to be the most unbelievable thing that God ever asked of anyone in Scripture. After all the years of his journey with God, Abram received the son promised to him by God. Isaac began to grow and develop, and at some time when he was a young man, perhaps a teenager, God commanded Abram (whom God had renamed Abraham) to go and sacrifice his son. After giving Abraham the son of promise, God commanded him to sacrifice that son.

When God first promised Abram a son, Abram and his wife did not have enough faith that God would awaken Sarai's womb, so Abram had a child by a servant girl. But later Abram and his wife trusted God for a miracle. The increase in their faith was a sign of God's plan of purification in Abram. God acknowledged Abram's spiritual growth by increasing his name from Abram (meaning "father") to Abraham (meaning "father of multitudes"). This purification of Abraham's heart revealed his ability to possess more blessing without being corrupted.

The promise is not the plan. The purpose of the promise is to motivate us to let God take us through the fires of purification. It is only after we are purified that the greatest blessings He has for us can be realized without corrupting our souls.

God's plan of purification will take us on a journey that never ends. He is always working to purify us through and through. Though God acknowledged Abraham's growth, the process of purification continued with the command to sacrifice the son that God had promised him. The depth of our sinful state is far beyond what we are able to comprehend, but God's plan for our lives is to continually purify our hearts. With each step of purification, God is able to release more of His promise into our lives.

The Lord's desire is to release every bit of His most supernatural plan into your life. This will bring Him glory and draw others to Him. But He must prepare your heart to make sure that His promises do not become your next idol. Though you mature and grow, God's plan is too big to be completed today, tomorrow, or ever—as long as we are in this earthly body. Every step of maturity will be followed with a command to kill the promise.

Valleys of tragedy will position your heart to choose between your love for God or the promises He's given you. Strife, stress, and conundrums will put you in a position where you have to choose between faith in God, faith in your own abilities, and faith in others. These hard choices do not come to you because you did not respond well in the preceding situations with God. They come to you because He is, once again, trying to move you to another level of maturity in order to release another level of blessing. His plan never ends this side of heaven.

Wouldn't it be nice if—after we've lived strong Christian lives for thirty, forty, or fifty years—God would say to his angels, "Okay, they have done well. Let's let them rest until they come to heaven. No more struggles for them." Then all the angels would salute their Great Commander, and from that moment on, we would have no more pain. Woohoo!

The only problem with that scenario is that it would indicate that God's plan for your life was limited. God would have to put up borders around His plan and His blessings for you. But God's love for you will never allow Him to limit the goodness He wants to do in your life. So the journey continues. God's plan for purification does not end. Struggles and temptations still come, but with your greater maturity, so do greater blessings.

"Early the next morning Abraham got up and saddled his donkey. He took with him two of his servants and his son Isaac. When he had cut enough wood for the burnt offering, he set out for the place God had told him about. On the third day, Abraham looked up and saw the place in the distance. He said to his servants, 'Stay here with the donkey while I and the boy go over there. We will worship and then we will come back to you'" (Genesis 22:3–5 NIV).

Here we see Abraham's incredible spiritual growth. God told him to sacrifice his son Isaac, and Abraham did not procrastinate. He did not even sleep in. No, he got up early the next morning in order to obey. There was no compromise or negotiation, only obedience and faith. As we witness God's plan, we see His servant changed from Abram to Abraham. He had changed from the man who had doubted and lied and sinned, to a man who was eager to obey God in this most difficult command, because he believed so strongly in God. Abraham said to his servants, "We will worship, and then we will come back to you." He had no problem giving priority to God over his son, because he had an enormous amount of faith in God and believed that He would keep His covenant.

When we are able to choose God over everything else in our lives, no matter how sacred something may be to us, God is able to do the most miraculous things in our lives. We must learn to choose obedience to God over obedience to our fleshly desires, our relationships, our entertainment, and our careers. These choices are key in moving forward in God's plan for us.

Too often, we do not realize the significance of each choice we make in putting God second or third or worse. We must train our minds to always see God's presence with us and to consider that our jealous and vengeful thought is a slap in His face, that our lustful thought is seductive adultery committed right before His eyes. When we lose sight of His presence with us, we easily insult Him without any thought of regret. He must become the love—*the* love—of our lives, with everything else being a distant second.

"By faith Abraham, when God tested him, offered Isaac as a sacrifice. He who had received the promises was about to sacrifice his one and only son, even though God had said to him, 'It is through Isaac that your offspring will be reckoned.' Abraham reasoned that God could raise the dead, and figuratively speaking, he did receive Isaac back from death" (Hebrews 11:17–19 NIV).

The New Testament gives us insight into Abraham's ability to obey when asked to sacrifice his son. He knew that if God could bring forth the miracle of Isaac once, He could do it again. This is the faith, the purity of heart, that frees God to release so much more into our lives. This is God's plan. This is the purpose of the journey of life. Every call for increased faith requires the sacrifice of yesterday's blessing.

I want to encourage you to take heart. Get up early in the morning. Do not procrastinate. Don't try to negotiate with God. Just obey. He is able to save, protect, and renew. The whole message of the gospel, from the flood to the cross, is the resurrection power of God. What we sacrifice to Him is placed in His hands, only to be brought back to life. Yesterday's sacrifice will become tomorrow's promise.

Abraham took the wood for the burnt offering and placed it on his son Isaac, and he himself carried the fire and the knife. As the two of them went on together, Isaac spoke up and said to his father Abraham, "Father?"

"Yes, my son?" Abraham replied.

"The fire and wood are here," Isaac said, "but where is the lamb for the burnt offering?"

Abraham answered, "God himself will provide the lamb for the burnt offering, my son." And the two of them went on together.

When they reached the place God had told him about, Abraham built an altar there and arranged the wood on it. He bound his son Isaac and laid him on the altar, on top of the wood. Then he reached out his hand and took the knife to slay his son. (Genesis 22:6–10 NIV)

We must analyze this moment from Isaac's point of view as well. He was not a small child. He was a young man at the oldest and a teenager at the youngest. His father, on the other hand, was an old man. I fully believe that Isaac had to allow his father to bind him up like this. Had Isaac fought him, I don't think Abraham would have been able to tie him up and lay him on the altar. At the very least, Isaac could have run away.

But he stayed. Isaac trusted his father, and he trusted God. What a difficult command was placed on Abraham to sacrifice his son, but what faith is displayed by Isaac to allow it to happen! The faith of a father had been passed down to his son. Isaac would make mistakes and sin, just as his father had. But his faith, learned at an early age through his father, brought him blessings a hundredfold.

We cannot dismiss too quickly a God who has presented Himself as our Father. He is a generational figure, always looking ahead to the next generation. His plans for your life are not just for you but for your children and their children and their children. Imagine how much more blessed your children's lives will be if they learn a strong faith at an early age. Perhaps your children are adults, grown and out of the house. Imagine how, even now, their lives can be positively affected by a significant transformational faith in you. Imagine the impact you can have on your grandchildren.

God's plan for your life is too big for the years you will remain on this earth. His desire is to pass it down to your children and your children's children. Let His plan—your journey with Him to a purified heart—come to pass. Approach every situation, big and small, as an opportunity for purification.

Don't let the situation you're in overshadow God's purpose for that situation. You might be dealing with a crazy driver cutting you off or losing your best friend in a car wreck. God's plan is to mature you, to prepare you for greater things. Along this journey, you will struggle, weep, and fail, but through it all, the Lord will never fail you. He will keep His covenant.

You must keep preparing and protecting the sacrifices. Keep giving your life to Him every day, even if you messed up horribly yesterday. His grace will keep you on this journey. His plan for your life is this journey. He is moving you to a place you do not know, a place where goodness, mercy, love, and blessing will follow you all the days of your life. And when you leave this earth, the blessings will pass down to your children.

You are living today, not just for you but for the next thousand generations in your family. The journey is long at times, but God is always with you. May the God of peace purify you so that all the desires of your heart come to pass and your influence will never be forgotten!

"'For I know the plans I have for you,' declares the Lord, 'plans to prosper you and not to harm you, plans to give you hope and a future. Then you will call upon me and come and pray to me, and I will listen to you. You will seek me and find me when you seek me with all your heart'" (Jeremiah 29:11–13 NIV).

Made in the USA
Columbia, SC
22 May 2020